*A*
# STILL
*and*
# QUIET
# MIND

*A*

# STILL

*and*

# QUIET
# MIND

*Twelve Strategies for Changing*

*Unwanted Thoughts*

# ESTHER SMITH

P U B L I S H I N G
P.O. BOX 817 • PHILLIPSBURG • NEW JERSEY 08865

Printed in the United States of America

**Library of Congress Cataloging-in-Publication Data**

Names: Smith, Esther (Biblical Counselor), author.
Title: A still and quiet mind : twelve strategies for changing unwanted thoughts / Esther Smith.
Description: Phillipsburg, New Jersey : P&R Publishing, [2022] | Includes bibliographical references. | Summary: "Do you experience unwanted thoughts that you can't shake? Learn how to use biblically faithful strategies to overcome a variety of different thought struggles and live at peace"-- Provided by publisher.
Identifiers: LCCN 2021048178 | ISBN 9781629959214 (paperback) | ISBN 9781629959221 (epub)
Subjects: LCSH: Thought and thinking--Religious aspects--Christianity. | Habit breaking--Religious aspects--Christianity.
Classification: LCC BV4598.4 .S65 2022 | DDC 152.3/3--dc23/eng/20211130
LC record available at https://lccn.loc.gov/2021048178

To those who have trusted me
with their deepest unwanted thoughts
and taught me how we can courageously work toward
quieting our minds

# Contents

# Introduction

# A LOUD AND RESTLESS MIND

*Why does God hate me?*

It's not a thought you want to have in the middle of the night, but there I was. Sitting in the bathroom unable to sleep, my head dropped into my hands. Frustration flooded my face, and I felt my stomach turn. *Why does God hate me?*

For several months, I had experienced head and neck pain that felt all-consuming. By day, I struggled to sit upright or concentrate. As evening approached, the pain only intensified. By 7 p.m., I had curled up in bed trying to sleep the burning sensation away, but the hours dragged on without relief. Physical pain was a familiar struggle for me, but this neck problem was new. I didn't want to deal with it. I was done. Yet another sleepless night without relief was too much. *Why me? What is wrong with me? Why does God hate me?*

Even as these thoughts raced through my mind, I could have quoted half a dozen Scripture passages about God's love for me. Every rational part of me would have told anyone who asked that, yes, of course God loves me. But despite my rational knowledge and theological convictions, my uncontrolled pain felt like proof that God's love was a lie. Unwanted thoughts that painted God as

9

uncaring and hateful materialized out of the dark. I *knew* God was loving. He didn't *feel* loving. What was I to do with the dissonance that had settled deep in my soul?

I had a few options. I could become alarmed that my theology was in danger. *How can you doubt the Word of God that speaks over and over again of his love for you?* I could berate myself for allowing such an unbiblical thought to come to mind. *How can you think such things? How ungrateful! Do you realize what Christ has done for you?* Or I could try to push the thought away and remind myself of how untrue it was. *No, Esther. Stop it. Of course God loves you.*

I'm fairly certain that none of these responses would have been helpful in my exhausted state. Wondering if God hated me was no insignificant thought, but even in that disoriented moment, I realized that the thought didn't need to be a big deal right then. Not at midnight. What I really needed was sleep. So I walked back to bed and plugged in a heating pad. Lying down on the comforting warmth, I set the unwanted thought aside. I took in several deep breaths, closed my eyes, and focused on the weight of my body as it began to relax.

Each deep breath in through my nose filled my abdomen. Each slow breath out through my mouth settled me a little deeper into my mattress. I began to pray, describing what I was experiencing to God. *God, my neck is on fire. I hate this. I don't want to deal with this anymore.* My heating pad and deep breathing took my pain down the smallest notch. My honest lament calmed my soul. My tears stopped flowing. My anger began to dissipate.

I turned to a familiar verse that often gave me comfort in the middle of the night and began to meditate on it. "Wait for the LORD; be strong and take heart and wait for the LORD" (Ps. 27:14 NIV). The Scripture soon became synced with my breath. Breathe in—*wait for the Lord.* Breathe out—*be strong and take heart.* God did not feel loving, but if I waited long enough, maybe I would experience what I believed to be true. The longer I meditated on this verse, the more my body and mind began to calm. Slowly I drifted off to sleep.

The next morning, I revisited the thought that had intruded on my peace and theology the night before. Armed with strong black coffee and the strength that comes with sunshine, I was ready to investigate. *Where did that thought come from?* A memory soon crystalized in my mind. A Facebook post I had seen earlier that week had been lingering just beneath my conscious awareness.

An acquaintance had posted a story of her miraculous healing. After a time of prayer, fasting, and repentance, the chronic pain she had been experiencing since childhood had miraculously disappeared. The moment I read the post, I closed my computer and shut off my thoughts. *Of course. Of course she got better. I can't even think about that right now.*

My attempt at thought suppression didn't succeed as intended. Underneath the surface lingered an unacknowledged thought that God loved the person he had miraculously healed more than he loved me. The thought bubbled up at midnight. *God must not love me like he loves her. Maybe he actually hates me.*

Simply realizing the origin of my thought brought some clarity that helped me to investigate further. Remnants of a prosperity gospel had lodged themselves in my heart. This false gospel whispered in my ear that the Lord heals those he loves and hates those he leaves in pain. That he rewards good behavior with desired outcomes and heals only those who pray longer, fast better, and repent harder.

Over the next weeks and months, I processed, prayed about, and worked through this thought in a variety of ways. I can't say the thought never came to mind again or guarantee it won't ever arise in the future. What I can say is that many of the strategies I used that night and in the weeks to come have helped me to keep thoughts like this at bay when my circumstances feel overwhelming.

Instead of feeling alarmed when I experience difficult thinking, I have learned to slow down and observe my restless thoughts. I calm my body, call out to God, and meditate on Scripture. I get curious about where the thoughts might have come from and practice other strategies you will learn in this book.

## COMMON TYPES OF UNWANTED THOUGHTS

How about you? Do you experience thoughts you don't want?

Like me, do you ruminate on beliefs about yourself, the world, or God that feel true even though you know they are not? Like many people I meet, do you feel tormented by depressed, anxious, or intrusive thinking? Like everyone, are you uncertain about what to do with some of the thoughts that enter your mind?

For some people, unwanted thoughts feel like a mere annoyance. Other people experience them as problematic daily interruptions, and still others would describe them as a brutal and invisible form of torture. No matter the level of your distress, unwanted thoughts of all kinds often seem better kept inside. Perhaps you have the feeling that if you opened up about what went on in your head, no one would understand. Perhaps people would judge you or even think you are crazy.

No matter how stubborn your thoughts may feel, you are not alone. We all walk around with thoughts we just can't get out of our heads. Consider some of the most common categories of unwanted thoughts people experience.

### Worried and Anxious Thoughts

Everyone experiences worried and anxious thoughts from time to time. Mild worry over life circumstances may briefly appear. Anxious thoughts may cause heart palpitations and stomach pain. Full-blown panic attacks may lead to fears of dying. *What if I don't know what to say and look stupid? What if my baby gets sick? How will I pay these bills? Am I having a heart attack? Am I dying?*

## Self-Deprecating Thoughts That Assign a False Identity

Self-deprecating thoughts arise when we see ourselves differently from how Scripture describes us. *I'm not good enough. I have to be perfect. I'm worthless and I hate myself.*

## Depressed, Hopeless, and Suicidal Thoughts*

Life circumstances, difficult relationships, and dysfunctions in our bodies and souls can lead us to depression and hopelessness. *This is too hard. I'm not sure I can forgive myself. Nothing will ever get better. People would be better off without me. I just want to die.*

## Racing Thoughts and Incessant Mental Chatter

Sometimes it's hard to turn off our brains. There may or may not be anything upsetting about the content of our racing thoughts. Either way, we wish we could stop the incessant chatter. *I should cook lasagna for dinner. I can't forget to change the oil in the car. What should I be doing with my life? I just want to leave everything and never come back.*

## Daydreams, Fantasies, and Mental Pictures of Past and Future Events

We may rehearse mental images of past events that we wish had gone differently. Other times, we fantasize about an ideal version of the future or predict every disaster we can imagine. *I can't believe*

---

\* This book will not address suicidal thoughts in detail. If you find yourself ruminating on thoughts of death, reach out to a friend or counselor. If your thoughts turn into a plan to kill yourself, call 911 or go to the nearest emergency room. For further help, consider reading *I Just Want to Die: Replacing Suicidal Thoughts with Hope* by David Powlison (Greensboro, NC: New Growth Press, 2010).

*I said something so stupid in that meeting. How much better would life be if I had a different wife? I just know my son will get sick and die.*

## Irrational Thoughts That Don't Match Reality

We all experience times when our thinking becomes biased or impaired and we struggle to see certain situations or people clearly. Sometimes this thinking can become obsessive. In other cases, people experience delusional thinking that breaks from reality. *No one likes me. If I touch that doorknob, I will get sick. The FBI is following me.*

## Sinful Thoughts

Our sinful thoughts can be judgmental, envious, and bitter. Other times they are lustful, angry, deceitful, and prideful. *I hate him. One lie won't hurt. I'm better than all of them. This will be the last time . . .*

## Thoughts That Contradict Professed Theology

Sometimes our thoughts contradict our theology in shameful or anxiety-provoking ways. *If I just _____, God will accept me. Does God love me? Is heaven real? Am I even a Christian?*

## Intrusive Thoughts and Images

Many people experience shocking thoughts and images that seem to spontaneously appear out of nowhere. These thoughts are typically highly distressing and feel shameful to admit. Oftentimes, they revolve around sensitive themes such as violence, sexuality, and faith. *I could walk across the room and stab my daughter. I just had a sexual thought about my pastor. I hate God. What if I jumped off this building?*

## Thoughts Related to Traumatic Experiences

Trauma occurs when distressing events overwhelm our ability to cope. Following a traumatic incident, it's common for our thinking to become clouded by thoughts that fit into many or all of the categories listed above. Thoughts filled with shame, doubt, fear, anger, and sadness may linger just beneath our conscious awareness. It takes careful examination to realize they are coloring our overall mindset far more than we realize. *I am dirty. God doesn't love me. I'm going crazy. I never feel safe. Will the pain ever stop?*

## Unwanted Thoughts about Unwanted Thoughts

Sometimes our most distressing thoughts happen when we start to feel bad, guilty, or ashamed that we are experiencing unwanted thoughts. *God must be so disappointed in me for being anxious. I'm a bad Christian for being depressed. Why can't I just stop thinking that?*

Which category resonates with you the most? Many of these categories overlap, and you may find yourself struggling with more than one category at the same time. No matter the type of thoughts you tend toward, it's likely your efforts to find relief haven't been completely successful. As hard as you try, you can't stop thinking, feeling, or believing the unwanted thoughts that cross your mind. What should you do next?

## A MULTIFACETED APPROACH

There is no single magic solution to changing our thoughts. When unwanted thoughts linger, we need a multifaceted approach that draws on a range of biblically faithful strategies. I hope to offer such an approach in this book. While considering these strategies, I have found it important to keep the following principles in mind.

First, our approach to thought change should be faithful to Scripture. *All* of Scripture. Instead of relying on a handful of isolated passages, we should attempt to understand how thought change fits into the overall biblical narrative. This broader perspective compels us to look at our thoughts in light of who God is, what he says about us, and how he relates to us. It opens our eyes to see our thoughts in light of God's love for us and his plan of redemption for all parts of ourselves, including our minds.

Second, not all unwanted thoughts are the same, which means they should not all be treated the same. Strategies that work for mild anxiety likely won't be sufficient for thoughts connected to a serious trauma. If you treat intrusive thoughts with biblical guidance meant for sinful thoughts, you will get worse, not better. When painful thinking clouds our minds, we need a variety of strategies that address the varying causes and consequences of our thoughts. These strategies should take into account the influence of our bodies, minds, souls, and relationships.

Third, as we engage this process of change, we should be patient with ourselves. If you have struggled with unwanted thinking for a long time, it can be easy to berate yourself for not getting or doing better. Instead, I encourage you to curiously consider some of the reasons why you may be struggling to make progress. You don't need to fast-track your way to healing or relief. Getting upset when you are unable to change your thoughts builds up anxiety and frustration. These emotions then feed back into your thoughts, fueling greater levels of distress. As you read on, I will help you to consider some of the common reasons people get stuck. I will remind you over and over again of Jesus's love for you, which remains faithful before, during, and after your attempts to change.

Finally, as you continue reading, it's important to remember that none of the strategies in this book will change your thoughts on their own. Rather, the strategies I offer "allow us to place ourselves before God so that he can transform us."[1] Romans 12:2 teaches that we are transformed by the renewing of our minds. This renewal does not happen through willpower or even by replacing our thoughts with Scriptures. This renewal is a work God does in us as we are united with him and receive from him the grace and energy we need to change (see 1 Cor. 15:10; Phil. 2:12–13).

We are transformed when we stand in God's presence with unveiled faces—with intimacy and vulnerability (see 2 Cor. 3:18). As we encounter his glory, we are transformed into God's image, and this transformation "comes from the Lord who is the Spirit." Our thoughts are changed as we enter the presence of a good and loving Father who helps us believe the truth found in Scripture and who does the work of transformation for us. You will find that many of the strategies in this book are tools to help you enter God's presence. There, the Holy Spirit can take over the transformational work you have struggled to achieve on your own.

## TWELVE STRATEGIES FOR CHANGING UNWANTED THOUGHTS

Each chapter in this book will offer a strategy to help you with the process of changing your thoughts. We will start by looking at some general approaches to changing thoughts that focus on your relationship with yourself, God, the world, and other people. You will *examine* your thoughts through self-reflection (chapter 1), *pray* your thoughts to God (chapter 2), *rest* your thoughts in God's creation (chapter 3), and *disentangle* your thoughts in community (chapter 4).

The middle chapters will look at a series of holistic approaches to changing thoughts that focus on your mind, heart, body, and life story. You will learn to *focus* your thoughts on God's Word (chapter 5), *capture* your thoughts and heart with a right knowledge of God (chapter 6), *calm* your thoughts by using strategies that address the body (chapter 7), and *repair* your thoughts by inviting God's presence and God's Word into your story (chapter 8).

Toward the end of the book, we will discuss more specialized approaches to dealing with thoughts that can be especially problematic. We will discuss how to *set aside* your thoughts when they are connected to trauma (chapter 9), *dismiss* your thoughts when they are intrusive and obsessive (chapter 10), and determine those times when *medicating* your thoughts may be a good option (chapter 11). In the final chapter, you will consider how to *sit with* your thoughts when they linger far longer than it seems they should (chapter 12).

## PRACTICE THE STRATEGIES AS YOU READ

Some of the strategies in this book are challenging. Others are time-consuming. Some will seem so simple you may doubt they will be effective. Many will feel easy to skip. *The strategies will work only if you use them,* so I encourage you to consider your mindset as you continue reading. I hope you will read each chapter slowly, practicing the strategies in real time instead of resolving to come back later.

As you practice, the goal is not for you to do each strategy perfectly or to get anything "exactly right." Instead, simply experiment and notice what resonates with you. Some strategies will work better for you than others, depending on the type of unwanted thoughts you experience as well as your personality and preferences. If a strategy doesn't work or even seems to make things worse, feel free to make modifications to it that make sense to you or even pass on it for the time being.*

You can get started right now. Grab a journal or a piece of paper. Go back to the categories of unwanted thoughts listed on pages 12–15 and consider two questions. Which categories do you struggle with the most? What specific unwanted thoughts do you most want to change? Write down any thoughts that come to mind.

---

* This is particularly important if you have experienced trauma or if you are experiencing intrusive thinking patterns that may be connected to obsessive-compulsive disorder. We will discuss more specialized approaches to dealing with thoughts connected to these experiences in chapter 9 and chapter 10.

Once you finish journaling, pick just one of your unwanted thoughts. Hold it in your mind and simply allow it to be there.* Don't struggle against it or push it away.

*Pause to reflect*

Close your eyes and take a deep breath to help you to rest and feel calm. Breathe in through your nose and out through your mouth. Do this several times.

*Pause to breathe*

Begin to meditate on Psalm 46:10, which says, "Be still, and know that I am God." As you breathe in, remind yourself—*be still.* As you breathe out, remind yourself—*and know that I am God.* Do this about five times.

*Pause to breathe and meditate*

Repeating these words is not a mindless mantra. It is a purposeful remembering of the Holy Word of God. Be still in his presence. Quiet your mind with his truth. Then open your eyes and notice: What happened in your mind? What happened to your body? What happened to the unwanted thought?

---

  * At various points throughout this book, I will ask you to purposefully bring to mind some of your unwanted thoughts. If you are struggling with a thought that seems inappropriate to dwell on purposefully or feels too distressing to bring to mind, you can instead bring to mind a general awareness of the fact that you struggle with that particular type of thought.

# Part 1

# GENERAL APPROACHES
## *for Changing Thoughts*

# 1

# KNOW YOUR
# THOUGHTS

"Wouldn't it make more sense to do this exercise with my head facing forward?"

I was lying on my back, and my physical therapist had positioned my head for an exercise. I couldn't figure out why he had tilted my head to the side so that I was no longer looking straight ahead. Or so I thought. He laughed and said, "Your head actually is facing forward. It just doesn't feel that way because your neck is misaligned."

He went on to explain the anatomy of our necks and how certain problems can lead us to lose accurate awareness and perception of our bodies. He also had neck problems and described how he once walked into the office completely unaware that his head was tilted halfway down to his shoulder. A coworker pointed out his crooked posture, but his perception of being upright felt so real that he didn't believe her until he looked in a mirror.

We have all, on occasion, walked around like my physical therapist—unaware that our heads weren't on straight. Except often it's not our bodies that we perceive inaccurately in these instances. It's the true nature of our thoughts and minds that sometimes escapes our awareness.

People often say to me at the end of a counseling session, "I didn't realize I thought that until I just said it out loud." Other times they muse, "I can't tell if this thought is accurate or not." We all experience thoughts that lie just beneath our conscious awareness. We all, at times, think thoughts that are more inaccurate or unhelpful than we would like to admit.

## TWO COMMON TENDENCIES

Why do we remain unaware of our thoughts? It often has to do with our tendencies toward avoidance and overthinking.

Some days I like to shove my dark thoughts into a little box and pretend they do not exist. *Everything's fine. I'm fine.* For many of us, constant busyness and distraction techniques help us to suppress our actual thought patterns. We don't know what we think because we don't pause long enough to notice.

Other days, I like to spiral into an abyss of unproductive thinking. My mind wanders, and I barely even realize it is happening. *Hello, midnight! Welcome to my brain.* You might think constant thinking would help us to know our thoughts better, but often this is not the case. We become so caught up in our thoughts that we don't slow down to observe them. The speed, number, and intensity of our thoughts can make it difficult for us to gain an accurate picture of our thinking tendencies and patterns.

Are you an avoider or an overthinker? A suppressor or a spiraler? A lot of us are a combination of both, and it can be helpful for us to identify our personal tendencies.

## KNOWING BEGINS WITH OBSERVING

Changing our thoughts begins when we move out of these tendencies and get to know our thoughts well by observing them closely.

Imagine that each of our thoughts is a train traveling a set of tracks. Our natural tendency is to ride inside the train. We get caught up in whatever we happen to be thinking and let our thoughts control where we go. When we let our thoughts carry us along, it's difficult to change them. But we have a choice. We can exit the train. We can sit on a bench next to the tracks and watch each train—each thought—pass by.

Knowing our thoughts starts with observing them. With practice, it's possible for us to step outside the trains of our thoughts and watch them as outside onlookers. We observe our thoughts by allowing ourselves to look at what we are thinking without making judgments or trying to change what we find quite yet. Observing our thinking like this is one way we become aware of those thoughts that dwell just beneath the surface.

In their book *Untangling Emotions*, Alasdair Groves and Winston Smith suggest a similar method for approaching emotions. They suggest that, instead of prejudging an emotion, you should "look at it, see what you find, and *then* (not before!) decide how to respond."[1] We need to observe before we judge so we don't miss anything important. No matter how well we think we know ourselves, we can be certain that if we watch closely, some of the passing trains will surprise us.

Many Christians avoid this process of looking closely and immediately jump to judging and changing. You might fear that taking time to observe untrue, unhelpful, or unbiblical thoughts is counterproductive or sinful. But observing thoughts is not the same as indulging in sinful thinking or succumbing to an unhealthy belief. Observing closely before responding is how we determine the true nature and full extent of our thoughts. We can't change what we don't fully understand. The story I shared in the introduction is a great example of how important this is.

## PRACTICE OBSERVING YOUR THOUGHTS

Our thoughts come in two forms. We experience mental images and mental talk. Mental *images* are pictures we experience in our minds. These pictures may represent memories or projections about the future. They may be images of faces or places or of experiences we have had or anticipate having. Mental *talk* is the running commentary we hear in our minds. We might remember words that were spoken to us or make sense of something "out loud" in our minds.

Let me show you what I mean. Close your eyes and count to ten inside your head. Did you *hear* the numbers or *see* the numbers?[2] If you *heard* the numbers, that was mental talk. If you *saw* the numbers, those were mental images. Now, count one more time. If you heard the numbers last time, see if you can visualize them this time. If you saw the numbers last time, try to hear them this time.

How did that go? What did you notice? We each experience thoughts a bit differently. Some people are very visual. Their thoughts almost solely take the form of pictures. Other people may struggle to know what I even mean when I mention mental images. Their thoughts almost solely take the form of an inner dialogue. Many people experience a somewhat even combination of both. No tendency is better or worse than another. We are all just a little different.

Let's try one more exercise. We're going to try to observe these two types of thought as they happen in real time. Don't worry if this exercise doesn't come naturally. We're just experimenting, and this exercise can take practice. Close your eyes and let your mind drift wherever it wants to go. Notice what happens without attempting to change or judge your experience. At first your attention may be drawn to sounds around you. Then you may notice your attention rest on emotions or physical sensations in your body. Sit for a few minutes until you start to notice thoughts emerge.

Keep your eyes closed and observe these thoughts as a bystander. You are sitting on a bench, watching them pass by. Observe each thought closely by noticing and labeling it. Each time you notice a thought that forms as a mental picture, say to yourself *see*. Each time you notice a thought that forms as mental talk, say to yourself *hear*. Some of these thoughts may disappear quickly, and others may linger. Avoid any urge to push away or hold on to any one thought. Instead, after you label each thought, let it naturally pass through your awareness as you are drawn to the next thought, sound, or sensation.[3]

How did that go? It can be interesting to simply rest and observe the thoughts that cross our minds.

## KNOWING REQUIRES EXAMINATION

Observation is the first step of knowing our thoughts, but it is insufficient on its own. God invites us into an even deeper process that Scripture calls *examining ourselves* (see Lam. 3:40; 2 Cor. 13:5). Examination is one way for us to "keep a close watch" on our lives and our doctrine (1 Tim. 4:16). It is how we discern the accuracy and helpfulness of the thoughts we have just observed. Through examination, we enter the beginning stages of the change process.

We often think of examination as a process of searching our hearts for sin. But the goal of discerning our thoughts "is not to simply avoid the evil in this life; it is to learn what is good so that we might embrace and enjoy it."[4] Yes, one of our goals is to take sinful thoughts captive. But the larger goal of examination is for us to cultivate still and quiet minds filled with enjoyable thoughts that are pleasing to God.

## PRACTICE EXAMINING YOUR THOUGHTS

You can practice examining your thoughts by observing one unwanted thought you struggle with, looking at it curiously, and asking yourself the following questions.

### Question №1: Is This Thought True?

God directs us to think thoughts that are true (see Phil. 4:8). We can assess if a thought is true by seeing whether it aligns with Scripture (see John 17:17) and by asking people we trust if we are seeing things clearly (see Prov. 12:15). This is an important question, because we experience much heartache and trouble when we hold on to thoughts that aren't accurate.

Untrue thoughts about our identity pull us into despair. *I am worthless.* False predictions about the future and inaccurate assumptions about other people enslave us in anxiety. *I'm going to fail that test. She must hate me.* Wrong beliefs about God and our standing in the world leave us wallowing in hopelessness. *God must not care that I am suffering. People would be better off without me.* The first step of examining a thought is to determine whether it is accurate.

### Question №2: Is This Thought Helpful?

It's not enough to think thoughts that are true. We have to apply wisdom and sensibility to our true thoughts by thinking them at the proper time in the proper context and with the proper motive.

It may be true that you have a meeting tomorrow, but the middle of the night probably isn't a helpful time to ruminate on what you will say. It's true that you struggle with sin, but it likely won't be helpful to think about your sin nature over and over again when you are feeling depressed. It may be true that your neighbor has a beautiful house that you wish you had, but fixating on this truth won't help your personal sanctification. After you determine whether a thought is accurate, your next step is to ask yourself, "Is it *helpful* to think this thought? Is it helpful for reducing my suffering? Is it helpful for increasing my holiness?"

## Question №3: Is This Thought Appropriate to My Situation?

When a difficult thought arises, we should also remember that our ultimate goal is not necessarily to make our thoughts more positive. It can be appropriate and biblical to think sad, negative, unpleasant, angry, or fearful thoughts.

If a bear is chasing you in the forest, you will hopefully and appropriately have thoughts filled with fear. Those fearful thoughts may keep you alive. If you witness abuse, it is appropriate to have thoughts filled with anger. Those angry thoughts could lead you to seek safety and justice for the victim. If you are facing extreme trials in life, it will often be more appropriate for you to let your thoughts wander toward cries of lament than to force your mind toward positivity. Our thoughts should appropriately reflect our circumstances. Biblically faithful thoughts are sometimes difficult and unpleasant thoughts.

## Question №4: Is This Thought Complete?

Sometimes we assess a thought and find that it checks all the boxes. The thought is, indeed, true, helpful, and appropriate. But our examination should not end there. We still need to consider if the thought is complete on its own.

One reason we need this question is because we sometimes begin to think that half the truth represents the whole truth. In reality, "a half-truth masquerading as the whole truth becomes a complete untruth."[5] In your struggle with unwanted thoughts, what half-truths have you started to believe? Yes, it's true you are a sinner. But what gospel truth do you need to hold in tandem with that reality? Yes, it's true that you are suffering, but what truth about

29

God might be helpful for you to hold beside your pain? Yes, your problems may be too big for you to handle, but what encouraging words are also true about your situation?

Asking ourselves, "Is this thought complete?" often leads us to remember or observe thoughts we had forgotten or downplayed that are relevant to the situation. "This is sad" may be true, helpful, and appropriate. But "This is sad *and* God is faithful" is true, helpful, and appropriate and offers us a more complete perspective.

Here's another way to ask this question that I have found helpful. As you examine a thought, ask yourself, "And what else?" I learned this question from a wise counselor, my friend Eliza Huie.[6] When we ask, "And what else?" it prompts us to consider other questions: What other thoughts are true? What other thoughts are helpful and appropriate to my situation? What noble, right, pure, lovely, admirable, excellent, and praiseworthy thoughts am I missing (see Phil. 4:8 NIV)?

## INTERRUPT YOUR THOUGHTS IN REAL TIME

Knowing the right questions to ask is a good place to start, but the real challenge is to develop the ability to bring these questions to mind when we need them the most. We want to be able to interrupt our thoughts in real time with these questions. Here's what that might look like.

James is standing in the kitchen making dinner. A thought pops into his head. *No one likes me.* Normally he would hop right on that train. It would carry him unawares into spiraling thoughts of hopelessness, depression, and self-loathing. But this time, he steps off the train and looks at the thought curiously. He asks himself the four questions and answers them honestly.

*Is this thought true? Not completely. Some people do like me. My wife. My kids. My friend Ben. Most people when they first meet me. But* it's legitimately true that people at work seem to dislike me. It's so hard to go to work when the rest of my team ignores me and talks about me behind my back.

OK, what about helpful? Is this thought helpful, and is it appropriate to what I'm going through? Well, yes and no. It's not helpful to exaggerate and say that no one likes me. But it could be both helpful and appropriate to think about the fact that people at work are mistreating me so I can figure out how to respond to them. It's also understandable this is making me upset. I'm making difficult but honest work decisions that people don't like, and the fallout has been awful. Of course I'm going to have difficult thoughts about it.

Is this thought complete? Definitely not. People at work don't like me, but their opinion of me doesn't define me. It helps when I remember my family and all my friends who love me and appreciate me. More important than that, I have to remember that pleasing people isn't the goal of my life. I can't place my peace on people liking me. At the end of the day, I am to be faithful to what God asks of me at work and then rest in his love for me. God, can you help me remember that? I know you are here with me right now, and I am really struggling to not be so affected by this. Please help me to remember how you see me and let your opinion feel more important than what other people think of me.

Do you see how James used the questions to interrupt his exaggerated, black-and-white thinking with constructive self-talk? His self-talk then turned into prayer—an important step we will discuss in the next chapter.

## STRATEGIES TO HELP YOU TO OBSERVE AND EXAMINE YOUR THOUGHTS

Many people find the hardest part of this process to be remembering to stop and ask the questions. How do we remember to do this in real time? We remember by practicing. We practice with strategies that help us to observe and examine our thoughts until the questions turn into habits. Pick one of the following strategies to try today.

## Strategy №1: Journaling

Take about fifteen minutes to sit down and write whatever thoughts happen to be on your mind.[7] Sit down without any agenda or focus. Whatever pops into your head, write it down. *The dog needs to go to the vet. What will I have for dinner? I've been thinking about the Trinity and what that means for my life.*

Silly thoughts. Deep thoughts. Random thoughts. Observe your thinking by writing out your train of thought, wherever it goes, without trying to direct it. Afterward, read back through what you've written with the four questions in mind. Repeat this journaling exercise once a day for a week, and you will likely be surprised by the thoughts you find dwelling just beneath your conscious awareness.

## Strategy №2: Mental Reflection

Take intentional time to reinforce the four questions while you are lying in bed at night, taking a shower, or engaging in some other mindless activity. Allow your mind to wander, and observe your thoughts as you practiced earlier in this chapter. Notice each mental image and each instance of mental talk.

This time, instead of labeling each thought *see* or *hear*, ask yourself the four self-examination questions. You might choose just one question to focus on during a time of practice, or you might decide to use any combination of the four depending on what thoughts come up. There is no right or wrong way to bring these questions to the exercise. Just experiment.

Sometimes this will feel silly. Asking yourself, "Is this true?" as you think about what you had for breakfast may feel like a pointless exercise. But there is a point. You are forming a habit. The more you ask yourself the questions, the more effortlessly they will arise when you really need them.

## Strategy №3: Feedback

Sometimes, to truly know yourself and your thoughts, you need feedback from trustworthy people. Remember my physical therapist? He was so certain his perception was accurate that he needed a coworker to help him see things clearly. We will talk more about the importance of bringing other people into your thought life in chapter 4. For now, you may notice times when you ask yourself the four questions and feel stuck. When this happens, consider talking through them with someone you trust.

Other people can help you to discern whether your thoughts are true, helpful, and appropriate. You may especially need a trusted friend or counselor to talk to as you consider the fourth question—"Is this thought complete?" Perhaps there is an additional perspective on your situation or your thoughts that you haven't considered. Maybe there is an insight that is easier for someone with an outside viewpoint or different set of information to determine. Sometimes we need to humbly recognize that we do not have all the information and ask those around us what other thoughts we need to remember.

The more you practice these strategies, the more you will increase your ability to interrupt your thoughts when it really matters. Later today, you may get caught in a loop of anxious, worst-case-scenario thinking. *Everything always goes wrong for me.* If you have taken the time to practice, you may find yourself spontaneously pausing to ask, *Is this true?* Next week, an unwanted thought may come to mind. *I completely failed.* Perhaps this time you will stop and wonder, *Is this thought complete?* You have just created space. You have just created a foundation for all the other strategies we will use in the chapters to come.

# 2

# PRAY YOUR THOUGHTS

Prayer directs our thoughts and attention away from ourselves and toward God. David Powlison gives a helpful description of how our thought lives and prayer lives intersect in his foreword to *A Praying Life* by Paul Miller. Reflecting on prayer as a conversation in which life and God meet, he says, "The best our world has to offer is to teach you how to talk to *yourself*. Change what you tell yourself, and your feelings about what happened will change. Change your self-talk, and how you feel about yourself will change. . . . But Jesus lives and teaches something different. . . . He teaches you how to *stop* talking to yourself. . . . He shows you how to start talking with the God who rules the world, who has freely chosen to take your best interests to heart."[1]

*Stop* talking to yourself? This is not advice we often hear. We are more often encouraged to *change* the way we talk to ourselves by identifying the lies we are prone to believe and using self-talk to replace them with truth, as we did in the last chapter. This is helpful advice, but Powlison points out that, on its own, it is also insufficient advice. Self-talk leaves God out of the picture. We have to move beyond self-talk and invite God into the conversation.

If we aren't careful, our approaches to thought change can become rooted more in a cognitive behavioral theory of psychology than in Scripture. Cognitive behavioral theory teaches that, since thoughts lead to emotions and actions, you can change your thoughts and life trajectory through rational, truth-filled self-talk. Self-talk that is rooted in Scripture has its place. It's an important and biblical practice that forms the basis for multiple strategies in this book. We run into problems, though, when our biblical self-talk drifts from the relational context we find in Scripture. Changing untrue, unwanted, and unbiblical thoughts requires truth *and* relationship. For real change to occur in our minds, we have to engage with God through prayer.

I read Powlison's advice on our thoughts and prayer right before a speaking event and decided to put what he said into practice. What would happen if I asked my audience to practice talking to God about their thoughts? I asked each audience member to identify a difficult situation from their lives in the past week. Each person then considered the specific thoughts and emotions they had experienced in response to that event. To close, I led them through a time of guided prayer, inviting them to bring those thoughts to God right then and there.

As I observed the audience, it felt like God was at work. The room was silent and focused. When we finished and debriefed, people shared how God had powerfully met them as they prayed. Several people remarked that they thought they had already prayed about their difficult situations adequately. Yet praying their thoughts helped them to meet with God in new ways.

I think this time of prayer was helpful for several reasons. My opening directions included three central elements that I designed to help people pray their thoughts in a biblical way: I encouraged them to pray thoughts that were uncensored, I invited them to become aware of God's presence, and I asked them to ground themselves in God's Word. When these elements are present, prayer becomes a place where transformation can occur.

## PRAY UNCENSORED THOUGHTS

God transforms our thoughts as we speak to him in an uncensored way. Too often, we want to have the "right" thoughts before we go to God. Deep down, it's easy for us to believe our thoughts should be true, reasonable, and figured out before we take them before him. Often, this is not possible. We can't always change what we are thinking in an instant just because we want to. What's more, I don't believe this is what God asks of us.

Psalm 62:8 extends an invitation. "Pour out your heart before him; God is a refuge for us." You might compare pouring out your heart before God to pouring Legos out of a huge container. A mixture of plastic colors and shapes crash into an unsorted pile on the floor. Similarly, when we pour out our hearts before God, all our unfiltered thoughts and emotions rush out and collect in a pile at his feet. True and untrue thoughts. Beautiful and sinful thoughts. Helpful and unhelpful thoughts. All our thoughts are brought out into the open.

Before we change our thoughts, we have the opportunity to speak out loud everything we are thinking to God, even if we aren't thinking rightly. Praying uncensored thoughts is an important part of the thought-change process that runs parallel to observing our thoughts without judgment. It's important because when we try to edit unwanted thoughts prematurely, we haven't really changed them. We have just pretended to change them. Only when we speak aloud the thoughts we *actually* have—not the thoughts we *want* to have—can we work through them and get to a place where we are seeing clearly and believing rightly. What better place to continue this process than in prayer? Here, God is present to help us.

We see this in the Psalms, which demonstrate what has been called "pre-reflective outbursts from the depths of your being in the presence of God."[2] Psalm 77 is an example. Reading this psalm, we observe the pre-reflective thought life of someone who is struggling with difficult questions about God. The psalmist wrestles with what is true. *Has God rejected me?* (see v. 7). *Is God even loving? Can I trust him to keep his promises?* (see v. 8).

The psalmist has a purpose for speaking his doubts out loud and processing his incorrect thinking. As the psalm continues, we see that his questions and expression of lament lead him to remember how God has shown up in the past (see vv. 10–11). He then proceeds to meditate on God's past works, reminding himself that God is holy and great (see v. 13). It seems likely that the psalmist never would have progressed to this new line of thinking if he had pushed his initial, untrue thoughts away.

## PRAY IN GOD'S PRESENCE

God transforms our thoughts as we process what we are thinking while being consciously aware of his presence. The book of Job is an example of how this happens. Throughout the book, Job suffers terribly. His suffering understandably leads him to think inaccurate thoughts about God and the world. *Death would be better* (see Job 3:11). *God is my adversary* (see Job 16:9). *Prayer is pointless* (see Job 21:15).

It isn't until Job requests a meeting with God and enters God's presence that he is struck by the error of his thinking. Hearing *about* God didn't make a dent in Job's thinking. But seeing God with his own eyes? Entering God's presence? Experiencing relationship with him? Encountering his holiness? Read Job 42 and see how his untrue thoughts about God change in an instant.

Through prayer we come face-to-face with God and continue the work of examining our thoughts that we began in the last chapter. Self-examination of thoughts is completed when we look at our thoughts, look at God, and consider how God looks back at us.[3]

When you pray your thoughts, how do you imagine that God looks back at you? Psalm 139:23 offers us a picture. As we approach God, he searches and knows our hearts, tests and knows our anxious thoughts. He sees the offensive ways that are in us, yet still he chooses to lead us in the way everlasting (see v. 24 NIV). In other words, he sees our true selves and loves us anyway.

As you pray your thoughts to God, he looks at you with love, mercy, and compassion. His love does not materialize because you just had a true, honorable, praiseworthy, or pure thought. It does not disappear because you sinned with your thoughts or can't seem to escape thoughts filled with suffering. God's love for you is present in the midst of your unwanted thoughts. It is not a reward for changing them.

Look at your unwanted thoughts, and you will likely see your suffering and sin. Look at God, and, if you look rightly, you will see his love and acceptance. Look at how God looks at you, and you will see in yourself the righteousness of God (see 2 Cor. 5:21). It is then, when we see God accurately and see ourselves as God sees us, that we find the power we need to change.

Our thoughts are transformed not through force and willpower but through relationship and connection. God's presence is powerful because in it we encounter his character. We see who he is and what that means for our lives. Encountering God's holiness and grace is the motivation we need to move away from thoughts filled with sin. The stillness we find in his faithful presence calms our racing thoughts and worry. His compassion and love help us to believe the truth when it does not seem to match our present reality. We leave behind thoughts of regret as we receive his forgiveness. We find help for thoughts of hopelessness as we meditate on his goodness. Telling ourselves to think something different is inadequate. Encountering God and experiencing who he is in our lives has the power to change everything.

## PRAY GOD'S WORD

God transforms our thoughts through his Word. His Word is the truth that sets our minds free (see John 8:32; 17:17). Prayer begins with uncensored thoughts and moves toward the truth and help we find in Scripture.

We will talk more in chapter 5 about how meditating on God's Word transforms our thoughts. For now, let's consider two ways Scripture helps us as we pray our thoughts.

First, Scripture helps us put our thoughts and feelings into words when we struggle to know *what* to pray. The Psalms can be especially helpful for this. They are prayers that help us to bring all manner of thoughts, emotions, and circumstances to the Lord. When we are sad, praying Psalm 13 can lead us through our lament. When we have sinned, praying Psalm 51 can direct us toward repentance and renewal. When we feel joyful—or perhaps even more so when we don't—praying Psalm 145 can give us words of praise. When words fail you, pray through the Psalms. They will help you to know what to say.

Second, Scripture helps us to sort through the content of our hearts and minds as we pray. As you pour out your heart to God and bring all your thoughts out into the open to place them in a pile at his feet, you will see more clearly to sort through the mess. This is a good time to return to the four questions from the last chapter while you pray. Are your thoughts true? Are they helpful? Are they appropriate? Are they complete? These questions can help you sort through which thoughts you want to keep, which ones you should give up, and what new information you want to add to the pile.

If we don't use Scripture as our guide as we answer these four questions, we will find our truth somewhere else. We will look for it from influencers, from culture, from whatever opinion or belief helps us to most make sense of our current situation. As we pray our thoughts to God, will we find our ultimate source of help and truth in Scripture, or will we look somewhere else?

## GUIDED PRAYER CAN HELP

If we need truth found in Scripture and relationship found in God's presence to transform our thoughts, it follows that we should probably read our Bibles and pray more often. If you're anything like me, this is easier said than done. It's easy to forget, not make time, or feel too overwhelmed to begin. Life draws us in many directions. We get sucked into our phones, diverted by small children, and interrupted by our work. Anxiety, depression, physical health problems, relational conflict, and all other manner of life circumstances can make prayer difficult.

As I think about these challenges, I'm struck by the fact that Jesus guided people through prayer (see Luke 11:1–4). Instead of telling his disciples to go and pray more, he stayed with them and told them what to say. Guided prayers lead us toward what might be helpful for us to pray about. They can help us to focus when prayer feels difficult.

In a moment, I am going to lead you through a guided prayer that will help you to bring your thoughts to God. Entering his presence will provide the opportunity for you to ask him to help you to transform your thoughts. Our thoughts are often responses to our circumstances, so you will start the prayer by identifying a challenging situation that has negatively impacted your thought life.

I encourage you to use this prayer right now as it is intended instead of just skimming or reading through it without pausing to speak to God. If someone happens to be nearby, you can ask that person to read the script to you out loud. You can also read through on your own and close your eyes at each instruction to pause.

## A GUIDED PRAYER FOR TRANSFORMING THOUGHTS

Go ahead and settle into a comfortable position. If someone is reading this to you out loud, you might choose to close your eyes. If you are reading on your own, take a moment to distance your mind from the distractions around you.

When you feel settled and ready, think back over the past week to find a starting point for your prayer. Identify one specific difficult situation that happened recently that you are still wrestling with. Picture it in your mind. Where were you? What were you doing? Who else was present?

*Pause briefly to remember*

As you continue, there may be moments when you find it difficult to concentrate. You may find your thoughts drifting to what you need to do later today or find yourself fixating on something that is troubling you. If this happens, just know it is normal. Simply notice where your thoughts want to drift and gently bring your attention back to your prayer.

Allow your mind to once again picture the situation you identified. As the situation unfolded, what thoughts raced through your head? Identify a few of the thoughts that were forefront in your mind.

*Pause briefly to remember*

Now, still imagining yourself back in the situation, remember what you were feeling. What one or two emotions were strongest?

*Pause briefly to remember*

Begin to transition from thinking about your thoughts and emotions to bringing them before God. Psalm 62 encourages you to pour out your heart to God. This means telling him what you are thinking and feeling and how you are struggling. Take some time right now to speak to him as you would to a friend. Don't censor yourself. Don't try to bring the "right" thoughts to him or the thoughts you think you should have. Tell him the thoughts that are actually there.

*Pause to pray*

Take a moment to remind yourself that God is present. He is right here with you in the room. Psalm 46 says that God is your refuge and strength, a very present help in times of trouble. No matter what thoughts or emotions you are experiencing, allow yourself to become aware that God is with you. Meditate on God as your present help.

*Pause to pray*

As you continue to process your thoughts with God, talk with him about the first three self-examination questions. *Are my thoughts true? Are they helpful? Are they appropriate to my situation?* Let Scripture guide you. Psalm 119 reminds us that God's Word is a lamp to our feet and a light to our path. His Word shows us where to go and what to do. Are your thoughts being led by Scripture? If not, what truth from Scripture do you need to remember?

*Pause to pray*

Talk with God about the final self-examination question. Are your thoughts complete? Or have you forgotten or downplayed important truths that you need in order to gain a fuller perspective? As you consider this, think about God's character and your identity.

Consider who God is and who he says you are. Consider each of your thoughts in light of Jesus and what he has done for your soul.

*Pause to pray*

Ask yourself how God might be inviting you to act. What steps might he be inviting you to take as you respond to the truth he has shown you? Once you identify an action, hold an image of it in your mind. Talk to God about how you will follow through with it.

*Pause to pray*

As you close your time of prayer, commit to believing the truths you have remembered from Scripture. As you breathe in, pray—*Lord, I believe.* As you breathe out, pray—*help my unbelief.* Continue meditating on these words from Mark 9 until a sense of calm fills your body and soul.

*Pause to pray*

When you feel ready, take in one final breath. Let it out and open your eyes. What do you notice? How do you feel?

# 3

# REST YOUR THOUGHTS

I'm sitting outside in my favorite chair while I write. The sun warms my face while a strong breeze hits my body. The temperature is perfect. I can't help but pause from my writing to enjoy the simple pleasure of being outside.

I live in a suburban neighborhood, and it's surprising how much wildlife I notice when I stop to pay attention. A squirrel trounces by like it owns our yard. Two red-breasted robins fly past, a crow lands on our fence, and a yellow bird of unknown variety pecks for juicy morsels in the grass. A bumblebee lazily drinks from a vibrant flowering bush.

I've been stuck inside all winter, and suddenly—it's spring. I close my eyes and enjoy the surround-sound chorus of caws and whistles. The pleasant cacophony of bird calls is much louder than I realized when I was focused on my work. Good words and good feelings fill my mind and my soul. *Warmth. Peace. Stillness. Sunshine. Rest. Thank you, God, for this moment.*

I'm thankful for the break. Life is busy these days. I often spend the entire day working on my computer, only to find myself drawn to my phone every time I take a break. I love my work. I'm also thankful for the convenience, connection, and entertainment I find each time I open my phone. Still, the constant intake of information, data, and opinions sometimes leaves my mind filled with restless, racing thoughts by the end of the day.

Knowing my mind's tendency toward exhaustion, I purposefully look for moments when I can set my phone aside and step outside. I don't need to travel far. A few minutes sitting in my backyard or a short meander to the neighborhood park is often enough to help me to clear my mind. It's good to breathe the fresh air and allow myself to simply exist without doing work or consuming information. My mind is most at peace when I create purposeful space to pause in restful and beautiful outside places without the company of my phone.

I think these moments help me to put into practice Jesus's invitation to set aside my worries, stress, and fear. I look at the birds and the flowers and all he has created and thank God for his goodness and care for me (see Matt. 6:25–30). This is rest for my mind. It's how I pull my attention away from the exhaustion of worry and work and choose to meditate on the beauty and goodness of all God has created.

## REST FROM CONSTANT DISTRACTION AND HURRY

Our minds need rest just as much as our hearts and souls do. This rest can be difficult to find because many of us live in a constant state of hurry and distraction. We throw ourselves into work and schedule ourselves to the brim. We avoid silence and solitude and use digital technology every moment we are forced to be alone.

While I am quick to embrace the many benefits of technology, statistics force us to reckon with the concerning impact that smartphones, social media, and mindless consumption of information and entertainment can have on the state of our minds. High levels of smartphone usage increase people's likelihood of anxiety and their perceived levels of stress.[1] Experts have attributed alarming rises in teen suicide and depression in part to the introduction of social media and the smartphone.[2] Unchecked technology usage can disrupt sleep and decrease our desire to seek out in-person community. Without adequate sleep and people to help us sort through our thoughts, the process of change can become more difficult.

It's ironic that we often turn back to technology to alleviate our thought-related problems. Our phones have become "digital pacifiers" that help us to avoid difficult feelings and problematic thoughts.[3] I realized this tendency in myself when the Screen Time app was released on my iPhone. I was surprised by how much my phone usage increased on days when I was anxious. Instead of pausing to know my thoughts or pray through my thinking, I would reach for my phone and scroll.

Richard Foster has called the distraction of constant technology *"the* primary spiritual problem in contemporary culture."[4] The multitasking encouraged by internet-enabled technologies has hijacked our attentional capacity.[5] This makes it more difficult for us to focus for any length of time on spiritual disciplines. We have less space, desire, and ability to examine our thoughts in the solitude of our own minds. We have fewer moments of quiet and less ability to concentrate on bringing our thoughts to God in prayer for any length of time.

In response to our hurry and distraction, God extends an invitation. As I look through Scripture, I imagine him speaking these words to you and to me: Come away to a restful place (see Mark 6:31). Slow down and savor the beauty and goodness in the world I have created. Let me show you how it reveals who I am (see Matt. 6:25–30).

## COME AWAY AND GET SOME REST

When Jesus saw his disciples overcome by weariness from their work, he said to them, "Come away by yourselves to a desolate

47

place and rest a while" (Mark 6:31). Come away. It's a needed invitation. To come away is to separate yourself from something. In the disciples' case, they needed separation from the hustle of ministry. They moved away from people to an isolated place where they could be alone. They changed their location and context to better accommodate their need for rest and communion with God.

What about in your case? Consider what hurries and distracts you. What exhausts your mind? What puts your thoughts into hyperdrive? What blocks your self-reflection or comes between you and time spent praying your thoughts to God? What might you need to come away from?

For me, the answer is clear. My work hurries me. A constant intake of information distracts me. I read the news while eating lunch, listen to audiobooks while doing chores, and read books or watch TV in my spare moments. Text messages, video chats, meetings, and work projects fill my day. There is nothing wrong with all these activities. They are good gifts that often help me to make the best use of my time and mental energy. At the same time, too many of these activities without a break leads to information overload. My mind fills with restless thoughts that can distract me from looking at myself and connecting to God.

Incessant mental chatter.* This may be the type of thought I struggle with the most. The speed of my thoughts tends to correlate with the amount of mental work I do in any given season. My mental load follows me to bed, where I continue creating grocery lists, rewriting sentences, pondering work problems, considering how I will respond to a text, and reviewing my to-do list in my mind. To break this cycle, I need to purposefully step away from work at various points throughout the day. I need to come away.

---

* The strategies in this chapter can be helpful for any type of thoughts, but they may be especially helpful for the category of racing thoughts and incessant mental chatter that was listed in the introduction.

For me, coming away looks like purposeful times of solitude away from other people. It looks like starting my morning with God through Scripture and prayer. It also looks like purposeful times when I distance myself from information overload.

I first completed a digital detox after reading Cal Newport's book *Digital Minimalism*.[6] A few years later, I was introduced to the concept of reading deprivation in Julia Cameron's book *The Artist's Way*.[7] I have come to think of reading deprivation in terms of fasting from information. For a week in the summer of 2020, I stepped away from all unnecessary information. I spent a lot of time sitting outside journaling. I had more time to pray. Sometimes I didn't think much and just rested my mind. Other times, I searched my thoughts deeply. I learned things about myself I had not previously known. The true content of my thoughts and state of my heart became clearer.

Fasting from information is one way for us to come away when taking time off work is not possible and the demands of ministry and family can't be avoided. When times of solitude are few and far between, we can still reduce the surrounding noise.

I encourage you to try this type of fast at least once as you engage this process of changing your thoughts. You can do this by picking a time frame during which you will fast from all unnecessary intake of information. The time could be fifteen minutes, an hour, a day, or up to a week. During this time, you will avoid TV, music, books (except the Bible), social media, podcasts, video games, news, and all other forms of media and information intake.

Julia Cameron points out that stepping away from information in this way often frees up peoples' time.[8] Consider using some of this newly created extra space for the journaling, mental reflection, and prayer-based strategies we have already discussed. Then use the remainder of your extra time to slow down and practice activities that allow your mind to rest.

Pick up forgotten hobbies. Finish projects around the house. Set an hour aside for a walk or hike. Sit outside. Bake cookies and eat them slowly. Plant a tree. Play with your kids. Turn your attention toward savoring the beauty and goodness of all God has created. I'll give you some ideas of how you might do this in the next section. Let these times of reflective meditation on God's creation remind you of who God is and all he has done for you.

## MEDITATE ON GOD'S CREATION

The concept of meditating on God's creation may seem foreign or questionable to some people. However, this practice is found all throughout Scripture. It has also been detailed in the writings of the Puritans,[9] who wrote extensively about biblical meditation and believed it to be an essential part of the Christian life. They identified two types of meditation, which they called deliberate meditation and occasional meditation.[10]

*Deliberate meditation* is the more familiar practice of dwelling on truths from Scripture and considering how they apply to our lives. We will discuss this practice in detail in chapter 8. *Occasional meditation* is the less familiar practice of noticing your daily life and considering how it reminds you of truth found in Scripture. It is the informal, spontaneous, and imaginative ability to meditate on everyday moments that symbolize spiritual truths. Through occasional meditation, you notice God's works in the world and reflect on the ways God's created order expresses who he is and what he has done (see Ps. 77:12).

Jesus modeled occasional meditation when he used everyday examples such as bread, water, mustard seeds, pearls, and vineyards to illustrate spiritual truths.[11] As we go about everyday life, we will find abundant opportunities to observe God's creation in ways that spark a deeper understanding of what his Word means for our lives. Observing God's care for the ravens and lilies reminds us of his deep love and concern for us (see Matt. 6:26–30). Gazing heavenward awakens a sense of wonder at God's glory (see Ps. 19:1). Watching a colony of hardworking ants prompts us to consider our own responsibility to work hard unto the Lord (see Prov. 6:6). What other surprising reminders might we find if we slowed down and took the time to look closely?

To help you better understand occasional meditation, I want to lead you through some of my favorite ways to practice it.

## Taste and See God's Goodness through Eating Delicious Food

Let's start with a meditation you can try right now. Turn your phone off or set it on the other side of the room where you cannot reach it. Grab your Bible and slowly read Psalm 34:8–10: "Taste and see that the LORD is good; blessed is the one who takes refuge in him. Fear the LORD, you his holy people, for those who fear him lack nothing. The lions may grow weak and hungry, but those who seek the LORD lack no good thing" (NIV). Read it one more time, perhaps out loud—this time more slowly.

*Pause to read and reflect*

Once you have finished, get up and find something you enjoy eating or drinking. Take your time. Pour yourself a steaming cup of coffee or tea. Make a savory snack. Find a granola bar, a piece of chocolate, or a crisp apple. Or grab a cold, refreshing glass of water. Sit down somewhere with your food or beverage. Eat or drink slowly while doing nothing else. Make sure your phone and TV are turned off. Avoid any sort of multitasking. Appreciate and enjoy each mouthful of your food or drink. Notice any pleasant smells. Pay attention to its texture. Take in any enjoyable feelings of heat or coolness. Consider how each bite or sip hits your taste buds in a unique way.

*Pause to savor your food or drink*

As you savor the experience, taste and see God's goodness to you. Thank him for all the ways he meets your needs for food and drink and so many other things. Consider how you lack nothing. Recall the many ways God has blessed you as you have sought him out and taken refuge in him. Don't rush. Enjoy this time. As you finish your last sip or bite, pause to appreciate how you feel. Take a moment to thank God for the ways he met you in this simple time of meditation.

## Remember God's Care through Observing His Creation

Consider another meditation that may require more planning. If you have time right now, find a pleasant place to sit or walk outside. Otherwise, schedule a time in your calendar to go on a hike, sit in your backyard, walk through the neighborhood, or drive to a beautiful place.

Before you go, slowly read Matthew 6:25–30. Read it several times and think deeply about Jesus's words.

*Pause to read and reflect*

As you head outside, put your phone on mute or leave it behind. Then take a few minutes to ease your way into a restful headspace.

Are you facing any problems that require your immediate attention or that you cannot get off your mind? If you identify an immediate problem, allow yourself to look at it. Sometimes we need to acknowledge restless thoughts by seeking to understand them and looking for solutions to them before we can let them go. For just a few minutes, give the problem your full attention.

First, look at the problem closely. Examine it in detail, looking at it from every possible angle and every possible side.

*Pause to reflect*

Next, broaden your view. Look at the big picture. What other people are involved? To what places, situations, or other aspects of your life is this problem connected? Seek to gain as full an understanding of the problem as you can.

*Pause to reflect*

Is there anything you can do to fix this problem? What would it look like for you to seek first God's kingdom in this area of your life? Consider the steps you might need to take.

*Pause to reflect*

Once you have acknowledged what you can do about the problem, next acknowledge all that you are unable to fix or control. What parts of this problem do you need to release to God? Remember Jesus's words "And which of you by being anxious can add a single hour to his span of life?" (Matt. 6:27). God knows what you need. He promises to provide. Rest in this promise and make a conscious choice to set aside the worries of your day.

*Pause to reflect*

Replace the noise of your worries with the beauty of your surroundings. Remember what Jesus said about the birds of the air. "They neither sow nor reap nor gather into barns, and yet your heavenly Father feeds them. Are you not of more value than they?" (Matt. 6:26). Consider what Jesus said about the flowers of the field. "They neither toil nor spin. . . . If God so clothes the grass of the field, which today is alive and tomorrow is thrown into the oven, will he not much more clothe you, O you of little faith?" (Matt. 6:28, 30).

*Pause to reflect*

Keep these words in mind as you sit or walk. Intentionally observe the details of God's creation. *What do you see?* Notice plants, insects, and animals. Look far into the distance. Look up to the sky. Look down to the ground. When something interesting captures your view, move closer. Let the details of all God has made fascinate your mind.

*Pause to notice*

Notice your other senses. *What do you feel in your body and on your skin?* Notice the heat of the sun or a cool gentle breeze. *What do you hear when you pay close attention?* Listen to the birds chirping, the leaves rustling, and the wind blowing. *What do you smell or taste?* Inhale the aroma of freshly cut grass or the scent of wildflowers. Take a drink of water and notice its subtle, refreshing taste.

*Pause to pay attention*

Rest your mind in the goodness of God's creation. Search for beauty and color. What do you see that fascinates you? Meditate on how God meets the needs of his creation and on his promise to meet your needs as well. The goodness of God fills the whole earth. Be still and quiet for a moment and let your eyes, ears, skin, nose, and taste buds savor it.

## NOTICE THE PLEASANT PASSING MOMENTS OF LIFE

Perhaps you don't have time to step outside for a few minutes. Or maybe you wish you could sit and savor your food without being interrupted by work or small children. No matter how full your life may be, there are always ways you can slow down in the middle of your work and your everyday life to notice pleasant passing moments. I have provided a number of ideas to get you started in the examples below. Don't feel like you should practice all these ideas right now. You can familiarize yourself with these examples and come back to them when you need them.

### Meditate on Psalm 131:2 as You Care for Small Children

As you rock your baby or hold a sick child, dwell on these words: "But I have calmed and quieted my soul, like a weaned child with its mother; like a weaned child is my soul within me." Let your love and care for your child remind you of God's love and care for you. Imagine quieting your soul before God. Consider how the safety and security felt by the child in your arms mirrors the safety and security of your soul in God's love.

### Let Your Breath Remind You to Praise the Lord, Who Gives You Life

Close your eyes and breathe naturally. Notice what your breath feels like as it enters and exits your body. Focus more deeply. Where do you feel your breath the strongest? Let each breath in become an opportunity to praise the Lord (see Ps. 150:6). Let each breath out remind you that it is the breath of the Almighty that gives you life (see Job 33:4).

### Meditate on God's Provision as You Knead Bread[12]

Kneading dough provides an opportunity for meditating on God's provision. As you stretch the dough, pray—*give us this day.* As you fold the dough, pray—*our daily bread.* Or form your own meditative words to match the stretching and folding of your dough.

## Meditate on Water as a Symbol of How God Has Cleansed Your Sin

As you take a shower, wash your hands, or clean the dishes, recall how you have been baptized into God's family. Imagine being cleansed from all your sin through the saving work of Jesus.

## Use Your Commute to Discover Your Own Meditation

The next time you drive somewhere, take a break from music, news, podcasts, and audiobooks. Instead, look out the window and observe the passing landscape. What do you see? What do you hear, feel, and smell? In what ways can your intentional noticing of a blue sky, crowded street, light breeze, warm sunshine, beautiful landscape, or pungent smell point you toward God?

As you try one of the examples above or come up with one of your own, focus your attention in two directions. First, look for God in your experience. Look for reminders of who he is, what he has done, and what truths he might want you to remember today. Second, focus on the physical sensations of the experience. Savoring what we feel in our bodies during an activity increases our ability to access positive feelings and recall positive memories of the experience in the days to come.[13]

## COME AWAY AND REST YOUR THOUGHTS

No matter the worries or work you face each day, God extends a restful invitation to you when your mind grows weary. Separate yourself from hurry and distraction. Move to quiet places of solitude and rest. Find moments of stillness in the cracks of your day. Pause to look at your thoughts and pour them out to God. Then, rest your mind as you meditate on the goodness and beauty around you. Let the whole wide world remind you of who your Creator is and what he has done for your soul.

# 4

# DISENTANGLE
# YOUR THOUGHTS

A picture once hung at the counseling center where I used to work. The decorative letters read, "Thoughts disentangle themselves when they pass through the lips and fingertips."[1] A suitable quote for a counseling center. It's exactly what happens there. People come to an office, share their stories out loud, and slowly make sense of thoughts that had once stayed tangled in their minds.

Kept inside, our thoughts remain a tangled knot of hopes, dreams, fears, sins, sufferings, and good and bad desires. Self-examination, personal time with the Lord, and rest in God's creation are not enough to disentangle this knot. To see ourselves and our thoughts more clearly, we need the active process of speaking our thoughts to another person and receiving feedback.

If you aren't already having conversations like this or don't know where to start, you may want to invite someone to read this chapter with you. Throughout this chapter, you will find questions, prompts, and exercises that will be most valuable if you consider them with the help of another person. As you talk about your thoughts with a wise and caring friend, you will likely start to feel less alone. As you say your thoughts out loud, a trusted advisor can help you to become more aware of your blind spots and point out connections you were unable to make on your own. Together, you can start to disentangle where your thoughts come from and where they are leading you.

## WHERE DO OUR THOUGHTS COME FROM?

Most of our thoughts occur automatically. We don't make a conscious decision to think them the moment they appear. Many times, this means we aren't even fully aware of the thoughts we have been thinking until later. We are often even less aware of how much our thoughts impact our emotions and choices.

Consider Pam's experience with automatic thoughts. Pam texts her friend, and she doesn't respond. As hours turn into days, Pam's thoughts start to turn. *She must not like me. This always happens to me. Am I that unlovable?* The longer Pam ruminates on these thoughts, the more she is filled with feelings of sadness, hurt, and anger. She sends her friend a passive-aggressive message and lies awake that night waiting for her to respond.

Or the scenario could play out differently. Keisha texts her friend, and she doesn't respond. As hours turn into days, Keisha's thoughts start to turn. *I hope everything is all right. Maybe she is struggling with her new job. This season must be challenging for her!* The longer she ruminates on these thoughts, the more she is filled with compassion and concern. She brainstorms ways to encourage her friend and decides to send her a card and bouquet of flowers.

If we want to change our thoughts, one question for us to consider is why the same situation can lead to such different thoughts for different people. Why did Pam automatically think she was unlovable, while Keisha automatically wondered if something might be wrong with her friend? In other words, where do our automatic thoughts come from? Let's begin to untangle three factors that are involved in our automatic thoughts: our hearts, our bodies, and our stories.

## OUR THOUGHTS REVEAL OUR HEARTS

Everything we do, including the thoughts we think, flows from our hearts (see Prov. 4:23). Scripture tells us that both our good and evil thoughts arise from the good and evil that is stored inside us (see Luke 6:45). Our thoughts are never amoral, because "we are never removed from the obligation to love and serve God."[2] We engage the world as "moral agents" who are responsible before God for the thoughts we think.[3] This means we can know something about the state of our hearts by looking at our thoughts. Pause. How does that biblical teaching make you feel?

People often get stuck here. They look at their thoughts and start to worry. *If our thoughts reveal our hearts and my thoughts are terrible, then I must be terrible. These thoughts must mean something awful about me.* Every unwanted thought feels like a moral failure. The call to self-examination starts to seem like yet another opportunity for someone to make us feel bad for our sin. Feelings of guilt, fear, and shame begin to grow.

These feelings sometimes arise when we hyper-focus on passages in Scripture such as Jeremiah 17:9, which speaks of the deceitfulness and sickness of our hearts. If we read this verse and stop there, we will find ourselves stuck in one of those half-truths that becomes an untruth, as we discussed in chapter 1. Many Scriptures describe the purity, thankfulness, love, peace, goodness, and uprightness that fill our hearts as well (see Pss. 9:1; 119:7; Matt. 5:8; Luke 6:45; John 14:27; Rom. 5:5).

Many of your thoughts are productive, lovely, obedient, trusting, beautiful, and good. Your mind is a gift. Your thoughts help you to work, play, and connect. Your mind is a wellspring of art, a solver of complex problems, and an essential ingredient in your ability to communicate and connect. With your mind you understand the gospel, share it with others, and engage in worship with God's people. Godly sorrow, grief, and pain proceed from your mind as well. Don't miss all the good your mind has to offer.

As we keep looking at our thoughts, we will notice that some of them are sinful, but this should not lead us to despair. Instead, this should lead us to Jesus. As we will discuss more in chapter 6, holding the gospel next to each one of our thoughts frees us from spirals of guilt, shame, and fear. In our struggle with all our unwanted thoughts, even thoughts that involve sin, Jesus looks us on with love, not condemnation.

What do your thoughts reveal about *your* heart? The writer of Psalm 26 says, "Test me, LORD, and try me, examine my heart and my mind; for I have always been mindful of your unfailing love and have lived in reliance on your faithfulness" (vv. 2–3 NIV). The psalmist's confidence to invite God's examination doesn't come from his own faithfulness and purity. He is confident to invite God into his deepest thoughts and desires because of God's faithfulness and unfailing love toward him. As we open our hearts to God and share our thoughts with other people, we can be confident of this as well.

To continue the examination process we started in previous chapters, talk through the following questions with a trusted counselor or friend. Journaling through them is also a good option, but some of these questions will be difficult to honestly answer on your own. It will be most helpful for you to process them with someone who can give you feedback and encouragement.

- What good thoughts well up from your heart?
- What sinful thoughts are you prone to dwell on?
- As you look at your heart, is your first inclination to condemn yourself? Or are you able to remain aware of Jesus's heart for you?

## OUR THOUGHTS OCCUR WITHIN OUR BODIES

We often focus solely on spiritual- and cognitive-based strategies when addressing our thoughts. In the process, we sometimes fail to consider how deeply our thoughts are influenced by our bodies. We can't think without using our brains and nervous systems. We also can't think without our bodies responding to our thought patterns. Every single thought we have is connected to our physiological makeup in some way.

A biblical approach to changing thoughts should take into account the fact that we are embodied souls.[4] Our souls are one part of a twofold, integrated whole that also includes our bodies. Writing on the nature of man, theologian John Murray noted that "man is bodily, and therefore, the Scriptural way of expressing this truth is not that man has a body but that man *is* body."[5] And since we are embodied souls, "all the important theological dimensions of personhood (that is, soul, spirit, will, conscience, mind, heart) emerge or emanate from our physical beings."[6]

To address our thoughts by addressing our hearts is to attend to just part of who God created us to be. People often get stuck when they treat thoughts that have a physical component as if they are solely spiritual problems. Trauma, hormones, medications, and various medical conditions can exert a significant influence on our thinking patterns. Addressing these physical components often helps people to make progress when they have been stuck.

### Some Thoughts Are Physical Symptoms Created by Our Bodies

A person living with Alzheimer's disease experiences memory loss and a decline in his thinking processes that are caused by a physical condition. If this person begins to believe his wife is alive when she is really dead, this thought can be understood as a physical symptom that has arisen due to the way Alzheimer's damages the brain. Delusions are another type of thought that can often be classified as a physical symptom. When a person living with schizophrenia has delusions that she is being followed by the FBI, this thought is a physical symptom. Categorically, we should think of thoughts like these in the same way we think of other physical conditions such as blindness or the flu.[7]

## Other Thoughts Cause Changes to Our Brains That Perpetuate Those Thoughts over Time

When we repetitively think the same thing over and over again, this changes the structure of our brains at the neural level to more automatically bring that thought to mind. Our thoughts become habits that are reinforced by deep-rooted neural pathways. This does not mean we are powerless to change our thoughts just because they have changed our brains. It simply means we will have to be persistent as we work to wire new thought habits into our minds.

## Unwanted Thoughts Are Often Caused by a Combination of Physical and Spiritual Factors

When it comes to the many conditions surrounding our thought lives, we often won't know where the physical or spiritual ends and the other begins. People disagree on the exact role the body plays in various thought-related mental health struggles, including anxiety and depression. These disagreements are understandable. We are complicated beings. As we attempt to tease out the causes of different types of unwanted thoughts, what we want to avoid is any tendency to moralize suffering or physical symptoms.

The body is an intrinsically good creation.[8] No part of our bodies, including our brains, is the source of our sin or can *make* us sin.[9] Many thoughts are highly influenced by the body, and the suffering the body causes should be cared for, even when sin is present as well.

How has your body influenced *your* thoughts? If you have wondered whether your physical makeup plays a significant role in how your unwanted thoughts started or why you can't escape them, here are some signs that this may be the case.

- The thoughts appeared suddenly later in life and don't seem to have any connection to difficult circumstances you've experienced or sinful choices you've made. Unwanted thoughts that are connected to a person's mental and emotional health often appear somewhat gradually and may have an earlier onset in that person's life. The sudden onset of distressing thoughts later in life can signal possible physical origins, such as a neurological condition or infection.[10]
- The thoughts began after you experienced a significant trauma or when you were undergoing chronic stressors that may have impaired your immune system or put your nervous system into overdrive. We will talk more about how these changes impact your thought processes in chapter 10.
- The thoughts are accompanied by significant physical symptoms that seem to fuel them (e.g., insomnia, heart palpitations, headaches, appetite changes, digestive issues, lack of coordination, aches and pains, exhaustion, and restlessness). For example, anxiety may cause symptoms such as insomnia or a racing heartbeat, and these symptoms may loop back and make the anxiety even worse.
- The thoughts began after you started or stopped a medication. This suggests they may be related to side effects or withdrawal symptoms (for example, some antidepressants can cause suicidal thoughts[11]). Or the thoughts seem related to your consumption of alcohol, caffeine, or other substances (for example, anxious thoughts are a common symptom of alcohol withdrawal).
- You can think of other immediate or extended family members who have experienced the same type of thoughts. This can indicate a possible genetic component.

- You have been diagnosed with a medical condition that is known to impact a person's mental health and thought processes (for example, thyroid conditions, traumatic brain injuries, exposure to toxic chemicals, Parkinson's disease, chronic Lyme disease, and various autoimmune conditions that affect the nervous system can all cause changes to a person's thinking).

We often need help determining the extent to which our thoughts are impacted by our bodies. The best way to begin teasing this out is to explore your concerns in detail with both a doctor and a counselor.

## OUR THOUGHTS EMERGE OUT OF OUR STORIES

Untangling our thoughts becomes even more complicated when we consider how they emerge out of the overarching stories of our lives. Consider Pam's response from the beginning of this chapter as an example. Pam's thoughts reveal much about her heart. It seems that her friend's opinion of her has become too important. Instead of being guided by God's Word, she allowed her friend's actions to determine how she thought and felt about herself. Because of this, we might assume that Pam's automatic thoughts are signs of immaturity and unbelief. We might guess the best approach for changing her thoughts would be to remind her that she is loved by God. Perhaps this is true, and Pam may find this helpful. However, it's also likely there is more to the story.

People who think like Pam may have understandable reasons for this kind of automatic response. Perhaps a parent left during their childhood and repeatedly failed to return their phone calls. Maybe a friend ghosted them, and they are still reeling from the experience. Influenced by these underlying stories, someone's thoughts might easily drift in unhelpful and unwanted directions.

Our thoughts are situated within the bigger pictures of our lives. They are influenced by our past and present experiences and relationships. They are impacted by our personalities and the cultures we live in. Our minds are filled with information from the shows we watch, books we read, news we consume, and conversations we have. The thoughts we have in response to an event are not just about that one event. Instead, our thoughts often occur as that one event reminds us of many past events that have been stored away in our hearts, bodies, and minds.

How has your story shaped *your* thoughts? Many of us have significant memories and experiences that continue to impact us more than we realize. We will talk about this more in chapter 8, but you can begin exploring this idea now.

You can do this by creating a timeline of your life. This can be as simple as writing out a list of important life events in a journal or on a piece of paper. Starting from the earliest memory you can recall to the present day, consider the key events that have shaped you. Write down any event, good or bad, that you consider important, significant, or shaping, no matter how small. Once you complete your timeline, review it with someone, taking time to go over the following questions.

- When did your unwanted thoughts start?
- What was happening in your life at that time?
- What life experiences and relationships have most impacted your thought life?

## WHERE DO AUTOMATIC THOUGHTS LEAD US?

We have just seen that our thoughts arise as our hearts, minds, and bodies seek to make sense of our past and present experiences. Our thoughts then impact our emotions. Our emotions and thoughts intertwine to influence our actions and our responses to the people and circumstances around us. Our actions affect our relationships and the direction of our lives. In reality, this process happens in complicated ways, but we can simplify it like this: *experiences* lead to *thoughts,* which lead to *emotions,* which lead to a *response.* You can go back and reread Pam's and Keisha's stories to see two examples of how this process can play out.

Considering that this is a common path we repeatedly follow, it makes sense that God changes us into new people by renewing our minds and changing the way we think (see Rom. 12:2). Change is initiated when we notice what we are thinking. Instead of staying seated on the train of our thoughts and letting our automatic thoughts drive us, we step off the train and pull up a seat. As we do, we ask someone to sit next to us so we can observe our thoughts together. Together, we watch to see where our thoughts are leading us and consider what changes to our thinking patterns this compels us to make.

Consider where your thoughts are leading you by bringing one of your unwanted thoughts to mind right now. Once you have it in mind, try to identify the most recent time this unwanted thought came up automatically. What happened right before you had the thought? What seemed to trigger it?

Once you have a thought and situation in mind, use the questions below to help you step off the train and process what happened. If you are struggling to connect a specific unwanted thought to a specific situation, you can use these questions to help you process your response to any situation that happened to you recently. Don't be fooled by the simplicity of the questions. They often reveal surprising connections that were lingering just beneath your awareness.

- What happened?
- What did you think?
- What did you feel?
- What did you do?
- Where are your thoughts leading you?

## ADDRESSING THE FACTORS THAT
## SHAPE OUR THOUGHTS

At first glance, it often seems that our automatic thoughts appear out of nowhere. When we take a closer look at them, we begin to untangle where they come from and the factors that perpetuate them. We can now address the way our hearts (chapter 6), bodies (chapter 7), and stories (chapter 8) influence our thoughts and minds. We will start this process in the second part of this book, beginning with how we can control our thoughts and minds directly (chapter 5).

# Part 2

# HOLISTIC APPROACHES
## *for Changing Thoughts*

# 5

# FOCUS YOUR THOUGHTS

Close your eyes and think about a pink tiger. Try to keep the focus of your attention on the tiger for about ten seconds, and then open your eyes. How did that go? Were you able to stay focused? Now close your eyes again and think about anything *except* the pink tiger. Let your thoughts wander where they want for about ten seconds, but don't let them drift back to the tiger. What happened?

Most people find it much easier to think about the tiger than to not think about the tiger. As you closed your eyes for the second time and let your mind drift, it's likely the tiger popped back into your line of thought, completely outside your control. It's easier to focus *on* a thought than it is to focus *away from* a thought.

In fact, pushing thoughts away often draws our minds toward them. Studies have shown that using willpower to resist a thought may help to suppress it temporarily, but it is then left to linger beneath the surface and reappear more often in the future.[1] This is one reason our attempts to change our thoughts are ineffective. We struggle because our goal is to willpower our way into *not* thinking about something. Instead, something else needs to take the place of an unwanted thought and become the new focus of our attention.

Through the practice of meditation, we can increase our ability to focus our attention where we want. Instead of frantically trying to push unwanted automatic thoughts away, meditation helps us to keep truer, healthier, and more useful thoughts in mind.

## A BRIEF INTRODUCTION TO BIBLICAL MEDITATION

Meditation is the practice of contemplation or reflection. When you meditate, you focus your thoughts somewhere. This means that meditation is inevitable. The question is not *will* you meditate, but *what* will you meditate on? Will you focus on your fears, anxieties, doubts, or other unwanted thoughts? Or will you purposefully linger on thoughts that are true, honorable, just, pure, lovely, commendable, excellent, and worthy of praise as Scripture invites us to do (see Phil. 4:8)?

We have already talked about the practice of resting our minds through occasional meditation. Let's turn our attention to deliberate meditation—the more familiar practice of dwelling on truths from Scripture and considering how they apply to our lives.[2]

This form of meditation might involve thinking deeply about who God is (see Ps. 63:6–7), what God has done (see Ps. 143:5), or what God's law says (see Ps. 1:2). It can include considering our ways (see Hag. 1:5), thinking about heaven (see Col. 3:2), or staying our minds on the Lord and on our trust for him (see Isa. 26:3). You can deliberately meditate on any passage of Scripture by reading it slowly, dwelling on a phrase or idea in it that strikes you, and reflecting on what the passage means for your life.

## MEDITATION IS MENTAL EXERCISE

Understanding the basics of meditation is easy. Knowing where to begin can feel overwhelming. What passage of Scripture should you start with? How long should you meditate? What if you become bored, restless, or anxious? Not only is it hard to know how to start, but once you begin, the actual practice can feel uncomfortable. Even unbearable. It's hard to sit and intentionally think. Meditation does not feel productive. After a mere thirty seconds of meditating, most of us are itching to move on so we can do something that feels more useful.

Meditation is like exercise. It's good *for* you, but it doesn't always *feel* good. And, like exercise, meditation is something you slowly become better at over time. A person who is completely out of shape can't spontaneously decide he wants to run a marathon and expect this to be possible. Instead, this person might follow a program to help him to slowly build up strength and endurance over the course of a progressive schedule. Meditation is similar.

Your brain is like a muscle that needs to be exercised. Many people give up on meditation after trying it one or two times. It feels too hard and doesn't seem to produce the desired results. This often happens because people have unrealistic expectations. Just as you can't expect to feel great at the beginning of a new running routine, you also can't meditate twice and expect to be good at it. When meditation feels difficult and does not lead to immediate results, you should not conclude that it does not work. Instead, you should conclude that you are out of practice. Your brain is out of shape.

Regular meditation slowly strengthens your brain over time. A great way to ease your way into it is to use a guided practice, which I will offer you in a moment. Over time, meditation can become something you practice on your own more spontaneously and in your own way.

## MEDITATE ON PSALM 23

Grab a Bible and find a comfortable place to practice meditating right now. If possible, use a physical Bible instead of a phone or tablet so you don't get distracted by apps or notifications. If you can find a quiet place to be alone, that is ideal but not necessary. You can still meditate if people are around. Turn off your phone and other devices. If you need to keep your phone on, place it away from you where you can hear it but can't easily reach it.

Open your Bible to Psalm 23. Slowly read the whole chapter.

*Pause to read*

Once you finish, go back and read it again—this time even more slowly. You might try reading it out loud the second time, if that seems helpful. Notice what words, phrases, verses, or ideas stick out to you. What grabs your attention? What descriptions, promises, or images feel meaningful to your life right now?

*Pause to read and notice*

Purposefully become aware of God's presence with you in the room. Keep an awareness of his love for you in mind as you linger on whatever has grabbed your attention. You might choose to close your eyes or change your posture in some way. You might repeat words from the passage in your head. You might visualize some of the imagery and imagine yourself being led through green pastures or accompanied by God through a dark valley. Allow your mind to creatively stir your soul.

*Pause to meditate*

As you dwell on these words or mental pictures, consider how they might speak into your efforts to change your thoughts. What truths in this passage might bring freedom to your mind? How might you think differently if this passage were to truly sink into your heart? Don't rush. Take as much time as you need.

*Pause to meditate*

As you finish meditating, notice how it went for you. How did it feel to meditate? Did meditation change your thoughts *as* you meditated? Do your thoughts feel different *after* your meditation? You might notice a difference, or you might not. Either is OK. Simply take note of what happened. Then conclude your time by considering one or two actions this Scripture is inviting you to take. How will your time of meditation change the way you approach the rest of your day?

## ENJOY THE MANY BENEFITS OF MEDITATION

I hope you enjoyed that last meditation. Perhaps it offered you a pause in the middle of your busy day. Hopefully it gave you a sense of rest and peace, if only for a moment. Meditating on Scripture does not need to be somber or boring. It can be a restful and enjoyable experience. Meditation creatively uses our minds and imaginations to help us to know and experience the truths of God more fully. Through reading and hearing the Word, we intellectually understand and cognitively acknowledge what God tells us to think and believe. Through meditation, we dwell on what God says and begin to feel and believe deep down in our souls that what he says is true.

When meditation focuses on Scripture, it can also be a means for us to build greater discernment as we change our thoughts. When we meditate on Scripture, we are better equipped to answer the questions we considered in chapter 1. Is this true? Is this helpful? Is this thought appropriate to my situation? Is it complete? What good, holy, beautiful, upright, and pure thoughts am I missing?

Meditation is also a powerful means of slowing down our thoughts. This is something I, for one, desperately need. Many days my brain runs on overdrive. I jump from text messages to social media to emails to work tasks to taxes to thinking about what I will make for dinner to ruminating on what that person said to me yesterday. Many people live in a constant state of distraction, and over time this can erode our ability to deliberately focus on just one thing. We can change this with practice. Over time, regularly pausing to meditate strengthens our ability to slow down and choose which thoughts will occupy our minds.

## OTHER WAYS TO PRACTICE DELIBERATE MEDITATION

As you consider how you might incorporate meditation into your life, let me give you some additional ideas for how to get started. Don't feel pressured to practice all of them right now. You can simply familiarize yourself with these examples and try them later.

### Set Your Mind on Things Above

Scripture says that we should "set [our] minds on things that are above, not on things that are on earth" (Col. 3:2). One way we can do this is by meditating on heaven.

Close your eyes. Breathe a sigh of relief as you imagine a place that has no suffering or sin. Imagine worshiping God without the slightest hint of doubt. Imagine rejoicing without sadness, guilt, or shame. Recall any Scriptures you can remember that describe heaven. Allow your imagination to wander. What might you see, hear, feel, taste, and touch? What might you do? How might you feel? What thoughts might fill your mind?

### Give Careful Thought to Your Ways

In Haggai 1:7, the Lord instructs his people to carefully consider themselves—to consider their actions and their hearts. Pause for a few minutes to look inward and see what you find. What sins do you need to confess? What desires are present, whether healthy or unhealthy? How are your thoughts leading to your actions, and what do you want to change?

### Meditate on God's Love for You

Romans 8:38–39 says, "For I am sure that neither death nor life, nor angels nor rulers, nor things present nor things to come, nor powers, nor height nor depth, nor anything else in all creation, will be able to separate us from the love of God in Christ Jesus our Lord." Recall other Scriptures you know that talk about God's love for you. Visualize what his love might look like. Imagine the words God might speak directly to you to express how he loves you as you face the struggles you are going through right now. What might he say? How might he comfort you, encourage you, and show his affection for you?

### Meditate on What God Has Done for You

Psalm 143:5 says, "I remember the days of old; I meditate on all that you have done; I ponder the work of your hands." Recall a list of ways God has met your needs. Picture what happened, including the specific ways God showed up for you.

### Ponder Any Passage of Scripture

Pick a passage of Scripture that is relevant to the unwanted thoughts you struggle to change. Read the passage slowly. Read it again and notice whether any word, phrase, verse, or idea sticks out to you. Become aware of God's presence with you as you linger on what has grabbed your attention. Dwell on the truth of the passage and consider how it might change your thoughts. Remember God's love for you as you think deeply about how this passage might bring freedom to your mind.

## THE REGULAR RHYTHM OF BIBLICAL MEDITATION

Throughout the Scriptures, meditation is mentioned as a practice that is repeated often, within the context of regular rhythms. It is practiced day and night (see Josh. 1:8; Ps. 1:2), because we easily forget the truths of God and need constant reminders of his love and care for us.

Over the years, I have developed a somewhat regular practice of meditation that has turned into a habit for two reasons. First, I do it at the same time and in the same place every day—in bed right before I go to sleep. Second, I use an app called *Dwell* to guide me through the process. I put in my headphones and choose from various Scripture passages and voices to guide me.

Try meditating every day for one week and notice what happens. Choose just one of the meditations detailed above to go through each day, or download the *Dwell* app. You don't need to meditate for long. Starting with just a few minutes is plenty.

As you do this throughout the week, notice how it impacts you. Notice how you feel and what happens to your thoughts while you meditate. Compare how you feel and think before you meditate with how you feel and think after you have meditated. Consider turning the practice of meditation into a regular rhythm in your daily life to help you in this process of changing your thoughts.

# 6

## CAPTURE YOUR THOUGHTS

We are almost halfway through the book, and you might be wondering why I haven't mentioned what may be the most famous Scripture on changing our thoughts: 2 Corinthians 10:4–6, the passage that tells us to take every thought captive. We need this passage to help us to develop a biblically faithful approach to thought change; however, there is a reason I have waited so long to bring it up. Let's take a closer look and you will see why.

In this passage, Paul says, "For the weapons of our warfare are not of the flesh but have divine power to destroy strongholds. We destroy arguments and every lofty opinion raised against the knowledge of God, and take every thought captive to obey Christ, being ready to punish every disobedience, when your obedience is complete" (vv. 4–6).

Have you ever taken a moment to visualize the metaphors Paul uses in this passage? If you have never done this before, read the passage one more time. Then, close your eyes and imagine what you've read. What do you see? Paul presents two battlefield images. We are to demolish arguments and pretenses that are contrary to the knowledge of God like an army might pull down or destroy a fortress. We are to take thoughts captive and make them obedient to Christ like a soldier might subjugate or control a prisoner.

Don't miss the fact that Paul is describing brutal military operations. This is a violent passage that evokes violent images. War is not waged gently. Seizing a prisoner who doesn't want to be captured requires aggressive force. When you destroy a fortress, huge walls crumble to the ground. Visualize these metaphors for a moment and consider what Paul is seeking to convey about our thoughts. When I do, I get the feeling that Paul is urging me to enter a battle for my mind with the vigilance of a soldier. Armed with powerful spiritual weapons, I visualize myself seizing and destroying each unwanted thought that enters my mind.

At one point, I wrestled with what these images seem to suggest. These pictures seem to contradict the gentler, more calming approaches I personally find most helpful for changing my thoughts. Paul says to take *every* thought captive. Does that mean I should seize and destroy every unwanted thought that crosses my mind?

To answer this question, it's important for us to identify the type of thought Paul is addressing in this passage. Paul is admonishing the Corinthian church for accepting hostile reasoning against the Christian faith and holding on to thoughts that contradict Christ.[1] Their thoughts have an "evil purpose"[2] and deserve punishment (see v. 6). It's no wonder Paul evokes images of battle. God's glory and people's eternal destinations are at stake.

Paul is talking about sin and false doctrines. He urges us to seize and destroy evil thoughts. We should expose and tear down bitter, greedy, lustful, hateful, envious, idolatrous, and evil thinking. He instructs us to demolish false teachings about Christ and to believe the gospel. We should vehemently refute arguments and ideas that lead us away from the Lord. But not every unwanted thought sets itself up against the knowledge of God. Some unwanted thoughts are painful, yet still obedient to Christ. This passage is not saying we should seize and destroy every painful, negative thought that crosses our minds. Second Corinthians 10 is about sin and the ways it infiltrates our minds and beliefs.

A close reading of this passage should lead us to respond in two ways. First, we should take sinful thinking more seriously than we often do. Second, we should be careful not to turn this passage about sin into a one-size-fits-all solution every time we suffer with an unwanted thought. Instead, we should seek to understand some of the ways that sin and suffering intertwine in our thinking patterns. Unpacking aspects of this complex interaction between suffering and sin can help us to know which thoughts require us to act on Paul's instruction to take them captive and which thoughts might benefit from another approach.

## THOUGHTS THAT ARE ALREADY TAKEN CAPTIVE

We can't assume that a thought needs to be taken captive just because it is painful, upsetting, or unwanted. The distress level caused by a thought does not correlate with the sinfulness or virtue of that thought. Painful thoughts do not equal sinful thoughts. Pleasant thoughts do not equal virtuous or moral thoughts.

A sexual fantasy can be both pleasant and unholy. The painful thought of living the rest of your life without a loved one is upsetting, normal, and a sign of how much you loved that person. Taking every thought captive doesn't mean seizing thoughts that are distressing and negative and replacing them with thoughts that are pleasant and positive. It means moving toward obedient thoughts that reflect a knowledge of God.

Some of our unwanted thoughts are already obedient to Christ and already aligned with an accurate knowledge of God. Also? They feel awful. The thought of seizing and destroying them sounds nice. But what if our unwanted thoughts sometimes serve important purposes?

Our fearful thoughts sometimes keep us safe. Our sad thoughts often help us to grieve. Our angry thoughts may lead us to pursue justice. Painful thoughts of many kinds can compel us toward heartfelt praise, prayer, and worship. Unwanted thoughts like these are already obedient to God, which means they have already been taken captive. We don't need to take them to battle. Instead, we should use the strategies we have already learned to approach them with curiosity and calm attentiveness. Thoughts like these don't require fighting back. They need gentleness, hope, comfort, encouragement, and healing over long periods of time.

## THOUGHTS THAT TURN TO SIN

How do we know when a thought has turned into a sin that does need to be taken captive? Our thoughts become sin when we break God's law with our minds (see 1 John 3:4). We often can't control the thoughts that enter our heads. We *can* decide whether we will entertain them.* This is the difference between being tempted by sinful thinking and choosing to sin with our thoughts. The actual temptation is not sinful, but it is where the battle begins. Will we go there? Or will we mentally walk away?

Sin begins in the mind. Our minds are initiators of moral action.[3] Our lust shows our true adulterous desires (see Matt. 5:28). Our anger reveals our murderous intent (see Matt. 5:21–22). Out of our hearts come evil thoughts that can lead to all manner of sinful actions—"sexual immorality, theft, murder, adultery, coveting, wickedness, deceit, sensuality, envy, slander, pride, [and] foolishness" (Mark 7:21–22).

---

* See chapter 11 for a discussion on how this advice, and other advice offered throughout this section, is often inadequate for addressing intrusive thinking patterns.

My mind feels like the safest place for me to sin. I may usually act in ways that look good on the outside, but nobody can see what I choose to do with my thoughts. It's easy for me to think my sinful thoughts aren't a big deal because I don't have to deal with the shame of exposing them. But then I imagine for a moment. . . . What if my thoughts were broadcast on a screen to the world?[4]

Many good thoughts would appear—beautiful and joyful thoughts, as well as thoughts filled with holy pain and righteous suffering. But when I think about my mind being exposed, my attention is quickly drawn to thoughts I know are wrong. My thoughts reveal the sickness of my heart. My daydreams reveal my idols.[5] I am too easily carried away by thoughts that are prideful, judgmental, bitter, and self-indulgent. Painful conviction. I'm thankful you can't see inside my head.

Many of the strategies we have already discussed have helped me to deal with these sinful thoughts. Now Paul urges me to take another step. I am to take my sinful thinking patterns captive. When my thoughts lead me away from obedience to Christ and away from a true knowledge of God, my goal is to seize them and destroy them. I need to identify them as sin and tear them down. I need to refute the thoughts and admit the extent to which they are leading me away from the Lord.

For me, this often means I need to make a conscious decision not to go there. I can admit when a daydream is sinful and choose not to dwell on it. I can be convicted by Romans 2:1 and decide not to judge someone in my heart. I can recognize when I'm starting to think I'm better than someone else and resist the pull. I can identify thoughts that are filled with bitterness and envy and mentally walk away.

I have the ability to choose not to sin in my mind. When I am tempted, I can trust that God will provide a way out (see 1 Cor. 10:13). Yet I am not always successful at controlling my sinful thoughts. I know the good I ought to do and don't always do it (see

James 4:17). It's a lifelong battle that is complicated by the fact that many of my sinful thoughts are deeply entangled with thoughts of suffering. I examine my mind closely and see a messy, confusing, tangled knot of factors and influences. My thoughts have been impacted by major stressors, minor traumas, difficult relationships, and my own broken physiology. I'm not always certain where the suffering ends and the sin begins.

I think this confusing knot of suffering and sin is one reason we sometimes ignore or downplay the sin that dwells in our minds. Suggestions that our thoughts may be sinful make us defensive because so much suffering is present right next to our sin. We rightly don't want to equate the two or allow people to shame us for being in pain. We feel self-protective partly because we are prone to deny and downplay our sin (see 1 John 1:8), but also because we may have been hurt by religious admonitions to legalistically control our thinking patterns. In short, we don't like the way the concept of sin makes us feel. We don't want to feel ashamed. We don't want to experience discomfort. We don't want to feel terrible about ourselves.

When the invitation to confess sin triggers a desire to self-protect, this is often because we have lost sight of how freeing it is to bring our sins before the Lord. No matter what I find in my head and my heart, as a believer I can be assured that acknowledging my sinful thoughts doesn't open a door that ends in guilt, shame, or condemnation. It opens a door to liberation.

Awareness of my sinful thoughts should lead me to conviction and confession. As I confess my sin before the Lord, I am reminded that he who knew no sin became sin so that in him I might become the righteousness of God (see 2 Cor. 5:21). God's righteousness. That is my true identity. I can rest in the work Jesus has done for my soul. I can experience true freedom, knowing my thoughts do not define me.

It is freeing to bring your sinful thinking to the Lord.

## THOUGHTS THAT ARE FUELED
## BY GUILT, SHAME, AND FEAR

But what if confession doesn't feel freeing? What if acknowledging sin doesn't lead to liberation? What if it leads only to fear and further self-scrutiny?

Many Christians who deeply struggle with unwanted thoughts are prone to sensitive consciences, perfectionistic tendencies, and black-and-white thinking. They scrutinize themselves closely, examining each thought to see what they find. They develop a heightened awareness of their thoughts and what they imagine the thoughts mean about them. Their guilt, shame, and anxiety don't dissipate with acknowledgment and confession. They may even grow stronger. When this happens, several explanations are possible.

### It's Possible You Are Experiencing False Guilt
### over Thoughts That Are Not Sinful

An overly sensitive conscience can lead people to see every unwanted thought as a moral failure. Lingering thoughts of grief that don't turn to joy can start to feel ungodly. The suffering associated with depressed and anxious thoughts is sometimes mistaken for sin. A struggle to change thoughts after experiencing trauma can look like a stubborn unwillingness to believe the truth of Scripture (more on trauma in chapter 9). Painful intrusive thoughts that are fueled by physical changes in the body can feel like the unforgiveable sin (more on intrusive thoughts in chapter 10).

When we see sin where there is no sin, it leads us to fashion standards for ourselves that God never established. When we fail to live up to these false standards, we are left to drown in anxiety, guilt, and shame. These feelings only serve to fuel the forward momentum of our unwanted thinking patterns.

## It's Possible You Believe Your Thoughts
## Mean More about You Than They Do

Unwanted thoughts may begin to color your sense of identity. Highly distressing thoughts feel like signs of weakness and failure. Sinful thoughts feel like proof that you are worthless or unforgiveable. Your inability to get past your unwanted thoughts feels like a symbol of how disappointing you must be to God. Fear and self-loathing intensify as your identity becomes centered around thoughts of suffering and sin instead of grounded in your unshakable standing as a child of God.

## It's Possible You Are Relying on Perfect Thinking
## to Justify Yourself before the Lord

Sometimes acknowledging and confessing our sin doesn't lead to liberation because we start to act as though we can justify ourselves through perfecting our thinking. We anxiously confess each individual thought of sin, sometimes ten times over, failing to see that this represents a heart set on saving itself. In doing this, we act as though we need to sanctify our thoughts to be right with God, instead of allowing our right standing before God to compel us toward more sanctified thinking.

Do you believe in Jesus and his work on the cross? If so, he has saved you and justified you. Your soul is safe with him. As Jesus is right now—glorified, righteous, and sitting at the right hand of God in heaven—"so also are we in this world" (1 John 4:17). This means we don't have to fear. We need not wonder whether our souls are on the line every time a questionable thought crosses our minds. We don't need to confess out of fear that we may be punished or lose God's favor in some way; we need Jesus's love to cast out our fear of what our unwanted thoughts might mean about us (see 1 John 4:17–18).

What does it look like practically for us to let Jesus's love cast out our fear? Sometimes, it means we become less concerned about whether each of the thousands of individual thoughts we have each day are sinful and more focused on the overall posture of our hearts toward the Lord.[6] Do we believe he loves us? Are we accepting the gospel? Are we resting in his work and his work alone? Our thoughts will become increasingly sanctified when we start to feel truly safe and unafraid because of the justifying work God has already done on our behalf.

## THOUGHTS THAT ARE CAPTURED BY THE GOSPEL

Only one thing can truly help us to overcome both our thoughts that have turned to sin and our thoughts that have become enslaved by guilt, fear, and shame. We must capture our thoughts with the gospel instead.

In the first chapter of Romans, we see that the most damaging consequence sin can have on a person's mind is to lead to a rejection of the gospel. Sin leads people to suppress the truth about God and exchange it for a lie (see Rom. 1:18, 25). Those who reject the Lord believe arguments and thoughts that set themselves up against the knowledge of God. Their thinking becomes futile and foolish (see v. 21). They deny God as their Creator, choosing to worship and serve false gods (see v. 25).

Even as believers who are held by Christ, we still fall into idolatry. We forget the basic truths of the gospel and seek peace of mind through our own efforts. But we won't find peace through staying focused on ourselves and perfectly changing our thoughts. We find peace when we set our minds on Christ and trust the work he has done within us (see Isa. 26:3). We find peace when our minds are captured by the gospel.

To those who are prone to legalistic expressions of guilt, shame, and fear when you address your thinking: Do you quickly forget that God is patient and forgiving? Do you berate yourself for not doing better instead of resting in God's work on your behalf?

Believe the gospel. As you examine your heart, remain aware of Jesus's heart for you. Rest safe in his love.

To those who feel uncomfortable at the idea of addressing your sinful thinking: Have you downplayed your sin in a pendulum swing away from people who have shamed you? Do you fear that acknowledging your sin will lead to discomfort or self-contempt? Believe the gospel. Regain a vision of how freeing it is to bring your sins before the only One who can set your mind free.

Jesus cares when we suffer from our thoughts and died for those times when we sin with our thoughts. This gospel reminder isn't something to tag on to the end of a long day. It's a truth we need to hold beside each thought we seek to change. Attempting to change our thoughts without holding the gospel in mind will plunge us back into a spiral of unwanted thinking. When we remember the gospel, even the most distressing unwanted thought dims in light of what God has done for us and what that means about us.

## THOUGHTS CAPTIVATED BY A KNOWLEDGE OF GOD

During my time in college, God captivated my mind with a desire to know him more. I can take no credit for the way this desire took me by surprise. I can only explain it as a gift from the Lord that I think back on and wish I could replicate. I suddenly acquired a voracious desire for the Scriptures and would often retreat to a cozy, closet-sized room on the floor of our dormitory so I could read the afternoon away.

During that same season, someone gave me a copy of *The Practice of the Presence of God* by Brother Lawrence, and I became intrigued by his idea that "we should establish ourselves in a sense of God's presence, by continually conversing with him."[7] To know God through reading his Word and inviting him into the mundane moments of my day—it felt like a necessary and worthy endeavor.

I can't say this mountaintop moment lasted for longer than a semester, but it did leave me with a taste of what it feels like to live out 2 Corinthians 10. It gave me a picture of how our minds can be captured and made obedient to Christ and how our hearts can be captivated by a knowledge of God that leads us to know him.

Paul's vision for the Corinthians and for us is so much bigger than getting rid of sinful or unhealthy thinking. He is inviting us to fill our minds with an understanding of who God is. We gain this knowledge as we study God's Word, but our desire in reading the Scriptures should not be for the sake of simply acquiring more information about him; rather, "we must seek, in studying God, to be led to God."[8]

We read his Word, meditate on who he is, and allow this to lead us into prayer, praise, and worship in his presence. Our aim is to become so captivated by the glorious truth of who God is that our attention has nowhere else to land. We can't help but gaze on his beauty (see Ps. 27). The glory of his presence drowns out all other noise. Our sin is vanquished and our suffering is soothed as we rest in the glory of his presence. We set our attention on God, seek his face, and become so enamored by his holiness, justice, goodness, and power that our minds can't help but be overtaken by his truth and his truth alone.

I think of striving toward this end and feel a mixture of hope and defeat. It sounds wonderful. It feels unattainable. My mind doesn't often set itself fully on God. I'm too busy. Too worried. Too overtaken by my suffering and distracted by my phone. Many days, God gets ten minutes of my attention in the morning, and that's it. Sometimes I forget he is there for longer than I care to admit. To invite him into every thought feels like a glorious impossibility. It's an ideal to imperfectly strive for, and I rest knowing that one day this will be our natural default.

One day our minds will naturally turn and fully attend to our Creator. Our hearts will be so captivated by worship of God that all else will fade. He will be the focus of our attention. Our thoughts will be overtaken with a desire to bless his name forever and ever. Until then, we turn our minds toward him the best our earthly bodies and souls can.

## A GUIDED MEDITATION FOR CAPTURING THOUGHTS

Let your thoughts be captivated by a knowledge of God right now. Settle in to this meditation by closing your eyes and taking in a few deep breaths. Then begin with a time of confession. Think back on your day and confess to God any sinful thoughts you find. In what ways have your thoughts sinned against God? In what ways have your thoughts sinned against other people?

*Pause to confess*

Psalm 32:5 says, "I acknowledged my sin to you, and I did not cover my iniquity; I said, 'I will confess my transgressions to the LORD,' and you forgave the iniquity of my sin." Open your Bible and read all of Psalm 32. Notice the freedom the psalmist experiences through confession. Leave your guilt with the Lord. Accept his forgiveness and mercy. Ask God to help you to feel his love for you.

*Pause to read and pray*

Turn your thoughts toward praise and worship of the Lord. Psalm 27:4 says, "One thing I ask from the LORD, this only do I seek: that I may dwell in the house of the LORD all the days of my life, to gaze on the beauty of the LORD and to seek him in his temple" (NIV). Pause to read the rest of Psalm 27. Then meditate on verse 4 or another portion that stood out to you. What might it mean to gaze on the beauty of the Lord? What would it look like to seek his face?

*Pause to read and meditate*

Turn your thoughts toward the promise of heaven. Imagine that day when your mind will be fully at rest. Only good, holy, pure, lovely, and beautiful thoughts will flow from your heart. Your mind will be filled with the praise and worship of your Creator. Revelation 5:13 says, "And I heard every creature in heaven and on earth and under the earth and in the sea, and all that is in them, saying, 'To him who sits on the throne and to the Lamb be blessing and honor and glory and might forever and ever!'" Close your eyes and imagine how that will be.

*Pause to meditate on heaven*

As you finish your meditation, remember that God is present with you. Allow his love to cast out any lingering guilt, shame, or fear. Rest with him for a moment. And when you feel ready, open your eyes.

# 7

# CALM YOUR THOUGHTS

"I don't know how to take this sensation captive. I try to fight back, and it's just not working."

A woman I was counseling who struggled with anxiety was describing a burning sensation she often felt in her chest. The sensation was always there, and it grew stronger whenever her anxious thoughts increased. The sensation was frightening. When it intensified, she worried that something might be wrong with her body, which only made her anxiety worse.* Sometimes the sensation would become so intense that she would begin to wonder whether it was sinful. She would tense against the feeling and try to make it go away. She would then feel guilty for, in her own words, not being able to take the sensation captive.

This conversation highlighted for me some of the confusion Christians can experience regarding the connection between our thoughts and physical bodies. It's not uncommon for people to wonder if highly distressing sensations in their bodies represent sinful expressions of their thoughts and emotions. It's also not uncommon for people to respond to these distressing sensations

---

* It's always important to have physical symptoms checked out by a doctor to rule out underlying health conditions—a step this woman had already taken.

by trying to fight them away, which typically makes things worse. In light of these common mistakes, I want to discuss a different perspective and response. The symptoms and sensations we feel in our bodies are not battles for us to fight but messages for us to attend to. Instead of fighting against unpleasant or painful sensations, we can calm the state of our thoughts by calmly responding to the state of our bodies.

In chapter 4, we discussed the theological need for us to address both our bodies and souls in this process of thought change. We also talked about some of the ways our bodies can cause and influence different types of unwanted thoughts. This chapter will further the latter discussion.

There is a reciprocal relationship between our thoughts and our bodies. On one side of this relationship, our bodies respond to the content of our thoughts with various physical sensations and symptoms. This means we can increase our awareness of our thoughts by paying attention to how our bodies feel. On the other side of this relationship, what and how we think are influenced by the state of our bodies. This means that calming our bodily responses through the strategies I will teach you can assist us in the process of changing our thoughts.

## OUR BODIES RESPOND
## TO THE CONTENT OF OUR THOUGHTS

Consider, first, the powerful impact thoughts have on our bodies. Our mouths water at the mere thought of something delicious we will eat later. Our faces turn red with embarrassment as we remember something we regret having said yesterday. And many distressing thoughts are accompanied by uncomfortable or painful physical sensations. Even Jesus felt his distress in his body. As he anticipated the pain of the cross, "his sweat became like great drops of blood falling down to the ground" (Luke 22:44).

You can feel the connection between your thoughts and bodily responses in real time by purposefully recalling a stressful situation. Think of something mildly stressful—but *not* traumatic—that occurred in the past week. Maybe you had an argument with your spouse, got stuck in traffic, or spent twenty minutes looking for lost keys. Close your eyes and remember what happened. What mental talk or mental images materialize? What were you thinking and feeling as it happened? Sit with those thoughts, feelings, and images for ten to twenty seconds. Then consider how you feel right now as you think back on what happened. More specifically, what physical sensations do you feel in your body?

If you pay close attention, you will notice your body respond to your thoughts. The physical sensations that arise as you think about this stressful situation may be subtle, or they may be obvious. You may feel a slight pressure in your chest or a sensation you can't quite explain in your head. Your stomach may turn, or you may feel a slight tingle run up your spine. Whether you are aware of it happening in real time or not, your body constantly reacts to the state of your thoughts.

## PHYSICAL SENSATIONS PROVIDE IMPORTANT INFORMATION

Perhaps this seems like interesting information, but you're not sure how it can help us. It helps because paying attention to our bodies provides information that helps us to become consciously aware of our underlying thoughts and experiences. Those of us who are expert suppressers may not even realize the number of thoughts and emotions we hide from ourselves. Thoughts that are not expressed often make themselves known through physical symptoms and sensations in our bodies. Panic attacks. Exhaustion. Stress-related chronic illnesses. Muscle tension. Stomach problems. Headaches. Each of these can be caused or worsened by unacknowledged and unexpressed thoughts that we store inside.

Sometimes I don't know I am stressed until I realize that I don't feel like eating—I've learned that losing my appetite is my first warning that I'm overwhelmed, even before any stressful thoughts or feelings cross my mind. The other day I thought I was feeling fine about a speaking event until a pressure in my chest alerted me to the fact that I was nervous. Other times, shoulder and neck tension let me know how upset I am about something when I'd rather downplay how much it is bothering me.

I am not the only one who receives important messages from my body. Over the years, many people have shared with me about surprising connections between their bodies and unrecognized inward states. Fatima didn't realize how much she needed to process her grief until she started experiencing panic attacks. It wasn't until his wife pointed out how his eating and sleeping patterns had changed that Ari realized how depressed he had become. Ginger experienced strange sensations all over her body that began to ease as she engaged in trauma counseling. Don's struggle with exhaustion began to relent as he sat with overwhelmingly sad thoughts and feelings from his past that he had long been avoiding.

Fatima, Ari, Ginger, and Don each realized something important. The physiological responses that accompany unwanted thoughts are not sinful responses that we are meant to take captive. They are flares that signal a need for help. Recall from our discussion in chapter 4 that our bodies are good creations and cannot make us sin.[1] Sometimes our bodies react to our sinful choices (see Ps. 32:3–4), and we can certainly respond to physiological sensations in sinful ways. But the actual sensations connected to our thoughts and experiences are typically involuntary bodily functions. Most often they are automatic responses to trauma, grief, danger, and deep pain that reflect the ways God has wired our bodies to keep us safe.

Our bodies speak to us. We would be wise to listen carefully to what they say. The more we pay attention to what our bodies are telling us and look for patterns in our experiences, the more we start to realize our true inward state. We start to see how certain bodily symptoms alert us to the depth of our pain and the true nature of our thoughts. Sometimes the distress and discomfort in our bodies compels us to deal with issues or thought patterns we would rather avoid. As symptoms arise, we can learn to stop tensing against these sensations to try to make them go away. Instead we listen to the sensations, calm them, and grow better equipped to address our thoughts as we rest in that calmer state.

## OUR THOUGHTS ARE INFLUENCED BY THE STATE OF OUR BODIES

Let's turn our attention to the other side of this reciprocal relationship. Your thoughts are influenced by the state of your body. The physical responses of our bodies to various life circumstances influence how and what we think. Our bodies tend to exist in one of three states at any given time, and these states impact our thoughts in different ways.[2] As you read through the descriptions of these states below, consider which one most closely describes how you feel right now.

### 1. A Calm State of Just Enough Energy

At their healthiest, our bodies are calm but alert, engaged with life but not keyed up. Our muscles feel relaxed, our hearts beat at a comfortable speed, and we are able to carry out normal eating and sleeping patterns. The sense of safety and security we carry in our bodies is reflected in our thoughts. Our thoughts are focused, move at a comfortable speed, and tend to be directed toward healthy, goal-directed activities. Emotions of hope, joy, and peace feel accessible to us. Our work and relationships can more easily flourish.

## 2. A Mobilized State of Excessive, Nervous Energy

At times, our nervous systems become mobilized and our bodies go into a state of fight or flight. We respond to life as though it is filled with danger. This is commonly experienced by those of us who are impacted by anxiety, stress, trauma, and some types of mood disorders. Our heartrates increase, and our muscles become tense. In ways that can be subtle or obvious, our bodies start to brace against life. Our thoughts move faster, and we find ourselves dwelling on what-ifs. Choosing where we want to focus our thoughts becomes more difficult. We may feel worried, stressed, or angry. When these thoughts and emotions are not handled well, they can negatively impact our work and relationships.

## 3. A Sluggish and Immobilized State of Decreased Energy

Our bodies can enter a third state of immobilization and collapse. We freeze in response to difficult life circumstances. This is often experienced by those of us who have depression or have experienced trauma. Our muscles may slump, our appetites may disappear, and our bodies and thoughts may move slower than normal. Feelings of sadness, depression, hopelessness, guilt, and apathy fill our souls. It may feel easy for us to distance and disengage from relationships and difficult for us to concentrate our thoughts on work and productive activities.

### NOTICE THE CURRENT STATE OF YOUR BODY

Our bodies are most prone to entering states of mobilized or sluggish energy if we have experienced a trauma or are going through chronic stressors. However, we all exist within these states to one degree or another as we go throughout life. Most of us make subtle movements between all three states multiple times a day.[3] This often happens outside of our conscious awareness. It is also possible to experience a mixture of more than one state at the same time.

Which state most closely resembles how you feel in this moment? Does your body feel nervous and tense? Does it feel frozen and subdued? Or do you feel a comfortable sense of calm? Because each of these states occurs on a continuum, their signs may be anything from obvious to subtle. Take a moment to notice what you are experiencing right now.

What physical sensations do you notice in your body as you sit reading? What emotions are lingering just beneath the surface? What thoughts are you most easily drawn toward?

With practice, you can begin to identify in real time how your body is responding to life.

## A GUIDED MEDITATION TO CALM YOUR BODY

The closer you pay attention throughout the day, the more quickly you will notice when your body becomes too keyed up or too slowed down. You can then use various strategies to move your body into a healthier state of just-right energy. One easy strategy you can try right now is a simple breathing exercise. You can use your breath at any time to help you to move into a calm state or to enhance a calm state that you are already in.

Begin this meditation by breathing in deeply through your nose while slowly counting to four. Pause for a moment and notice the subtle gap between inhale and exhale. Then breathe out slowly through your mouth while counting to four again. Try it one more time. Did you feel your body relax just the slightest?

Let's practice again. This time, rest one hand on your stomach and one hand on your chest. Many people have a tendency to take shallow breaths into their chests. Instead, try to breathe into your stomach. As you breathe in, you want to feel the hand on your stomach move while the hand on your chest remains still.

Your goal is not to breathe exactly right—breathing deeply into your stomach takes practice and can be difficult for some people. Simply experiment with it and know it gets easier the more you practice. If it feels stressful to try to breathe this way, simply breathe in any way that feels relaxing to you. Close your eyes and continue this breathing pattern five times. Notice what happens.

*Pause to breathe*

As you continue breathing, begin to meditate on Psalm 46:10, which says, "Be still, and know that I am God." Allow the words of this psalm to sync with your breath. As you breathe in, remind yourself—*be still.* As you breathe out, remind yourself—*and know that I am God.* Breathe in again—*be still.* Breathe out again—*and know that I am God.* Continue this meditation two more times. Notice how you feel.

*Pause to breathe and meditate*

Notice the natural posture of your body. If you are leaning forward tensely, allow yourself to relax back. If you are collapsed in on yourself, straighten yourself into a more open posture. Take in another deep breath, and as you let it out, allow your face to soften. Open your mouth slightly and let your jaw relax.

*Pause to breathe and relax*

Notice your shoulders. Pay attention to any tension or stress you are holding there. Take in another breath, and as you release it, allow your shoulders to settle. Acknowledge your desire to give your stress to God. Remember Jesus's words in Matthew 11:28: "Come to me, all who labor and are heavy laden, and I will give you rest." Match these words with your breathing.

Breathe in—*come to me.* Breathe out—*I will give you rest.* Breathe in again—*come to me.* Breathe out again—*I will give you rest.* Repeat this meditation three times.

*Pause to breathe and meditate*

Notice your arms and hands. Clench your hands for a moment and ask yourself what you need to release to God. Remember Jesus's words as he anticipated the cross (Luke 22:42): "Not my will, but yours, be done." Match these words with your breathing. Breathe in—*not my will.* Breathe out as you open your hands—*but yours be done.* Breathe in again, clenching your hands—*not my will.* Breathe out again, relaxing your hands—*but yours be done.* Repeat this meditation three times.

*Pause to breathe and meditate*

Notice your legs and feet. If you are seated or standing, plant your feet firmly on the ground. If not, move into a position where you can place both feet on the floor, or else visualize these next instructions. Psalm 61:2 says, "From the end of the earth I call to you when my heart is faint. Lead me to the rock that is higher than I." Gently push your feet downward, feeling or visualizing the ground beneath you. Then match this Scripture with your breathing. Breathe in—*lead me.* Breathe out as you relax your feet—*to the rock.* Push your feet and breathe in again—*lead me.* Relax your feet and breathe out again—*to the rock.* Repeat this meditation three times.

*Pause to breathe and meditate*

As you finish this time of meditation, rest with God for a moment. Set all thoughts to the side and sit in his presence. When you feel ready, bring your attention back to the room. What do you notice? What happened to the state of your body? What happened to the state of your thoughts?

## CALMING OUR BODIES HELPS US TO RETREAT AND REFLECT

For many people, deep breathing initiates an immediate calming response. Pairing deep breathing with Scripture meditation can be especially powerful, as this strategy simultaneously addresses both parts of who God created us to be. As you practiced the above meditation, it's quite likely you found yourself moving further into a state of just-right energy.* In this state, we find a place of reflection and retreat that can assist us as we continue the process of changing our thoughts.

Strategies that calm our bodies can provide a temporary retreat when it is wiser for us to deal with the root of our unwanted thoughts at a later time. You probably don't have time to deeply understand your thoughts in the middle of your workday, while you are helping your child with homework, or when you are listening to a friend in need. That's OK. Take a deep breath. Meditate on a favorite Scripture or a passage you read that morning. Set your thoughts to the side. You should deal with them later, but you don't have to deal with them now.

Other times, when we are in a better context for dealing with our thoughts, calming our bodies helps us to pause, which creates

---

* Don't be concerned if the deep breathing did not have a calming effect for you. There are many reasons why you might need different or additional strategies to calm your body. For example, both trauma and chronic pain can impede the calming effect of breathing on the body. As with every strategy in this book, your only goal is to experiment and remain curious about what works and doesn't work for you. Feel free to modify the breathing exercise in a way that feels good or to focus on other strategies that seem more helpful moving forward.

a better context for reflection.[4] Taking a deep breath can inter-rupt overwhelming thoughts, feelings, and physical sensations. As our nervous system moves into a state of just-right energy, we have room to pause and think. We have space to choose a better response. We are placed in a calmer mindset that enables us to better use many of the other strategies in this book.

# 8

# REPAIR YOUR
# THOUGHTS

When did it start? It's often one of the first questions I ask the people I'm counseling. When did the unwanted thoughts begin? You might not remember the exact moment the thoughts materialized, so it's OK if you need to think generally. About how old were you? And what was happening in your life at the time? These can be revealing questions. Unwanted thoughts often begin during stressful seasons of life. They are often related to difficult relationships or circumstances. They might be connected to a trauma, a crisis, or an ongoing struggle. Pick a thought, any thought, and you will likely find that it has a significant origin.

Sometimes we don't even consider that the thoughts we have today could find their origin in events that happened weeks, years, or decades earlier and could be healed when we revisit those events. It can feel as if things that happened that long ago should no longer affect us and as if, when difficult circumstances pass, the unwanted thoughts should pass with them. But this often is not the case. Our past experiences often have an unconscious impact on our present thinking.

In this chapter, I'll show you how to revisit past events and relationships to help you to repair inaccurate thoughts you are tempted to believe. To some extent, this process involves replacing false thoughts with true thoughts. But repairing our thoughts is a deeper process than merely replacing lies with truth. We are seeking to first uncover *why* we started to believe the lies in the first place.

Finding the "why" gives us a tangible starting point as we engage the thought-change process. It often leads us to people and experiences that deeply shaped us. Inaccurate thoughts often develop out of inaccurate understandings of our past stories. Our thoughts can be repaired as we reconsider past memories and relationships in order to explore the false messages that have shaped us, find God in our past experiences, and connect our lives to biblical stories.

## EXPLORING THE FALSE MESSAGES
## THAT HAVE SHAPED US

Jane struggles with a barrage of unwanted thoughts. *I'm not good enough. I never do anything right.* They arise each time she struggles to connect with new friends, every day when she fails to keep her house clean, and every time she scrolls through social media. The thoughts are at their worst when she considers her perceived failings as a parent. Unwanted thoughts intrude on her as she helps her kids with their homework, makes choices about discipline, and navigates the constant ups and downs of parenting four children. *I'm not good enough. I'm not patient enough. I'm a terrible parent.*

One day, completely overwhelmed and at a loss for what to do, she shares these thoughts with a wise friend who begins to ask her questions about them. A lightbulb moment ensues. Jane first heard these messages from her mother. Her mother would often berate her for not doing things right. A key memory sticks out in her mind.

When Jane was nine, she was helping her mother to bake cookies. She accidentally dropped an entire bag of flour on the floor, and her mother was furious. Jane still remembers the look on her mother's face as she yelled at her and threw her out of the kitchen. "What is wrong with you? You never do anything right! Leave the kitchen, and I'll finish this myself. It will be easier without you."

As Jane revisits this memory, she realizes it represents a theme in her childhood that has infiltrated the thoughts she now has as an adult. Her parents often yelled at her for small things. They often compared her to her more successful siblings and constantly made her feel small, insignificant, and worthless. Even though Jane can rationalize in her head that she is not a terrible person and that she does do many things right, she can never feel in her heart that these thoughts are true. The messages her mother spoke to her can't be easily replaced. They need to be repaired.

Our thoughts are impacted by the accumulation of our past experiences and relationships. We can know *what* is true from what we read in Scripture. Sometimes this information lands in our heads but doesn't permeate into our hearts. God often helps us to work through this disconnect by sending people and experiences into our lives that embody his truth.

Jane's ability to see herself accurately grows as she speaks to her friend, opens up to her husband, and eventually talks with a counselor. In these conversations, she experiences people who treat her as though she is worthy even when she does not feel that way. These conversations also bring back memories of other key people in her life who have not treated her with the same distain that she experienced from her mother. She starts to recall pleasant memories of baking with her grandmother, who never acted like she wasn't good enough and never became upset when she made a mistake.

One reason the process of repairing thoughts that are related to past experiences can be difficult for us is because our brains have an ingrained negativity bias.[1] Research shows that we have a tendency to pay more attention to negative events and messages than to positive ones. We hold on to lessons we have learned from slights, insults, betrayals, and abuse and forget the positive messages that we have also received. Our thoughts, decisions, and actions then become skewed in light of the negative messages we fixate on.

I imagine this is one reason God constantly redirects our thoughts and tells us what is most important for us to remember. Instead of allowing us to fixate on all that has gone wrong, all those times life didn't seem to match God's Word, and all those moments when it felt like God didn't show up, Scripture points our thoughts in a new direction. It calls us to remember, instead, God's wonders, deeds, and miracles (see Pss. 77:11; 105:5). To remember how he led us through suffering and pain, never leaving our side (see Deut. 8:2). To remember all that Jesus has said and done (see John 14:26). To remember his body and blood poured out for us (see 1 Cor. 11:24–25).

The goal of remembering is not to forget the negative and focus only on the positive. The goal is for us to move out of our negativity bias and honestly look at our memories and experiences as they actually happened. Instead of skewing our thoughts in one direction, we honestly acknowledge the negative messages that have impacted our thoughts while also purposefully drawing on the healthy messages we so easily forget.

## FINDING GOD IN OUR PAST EXPERIENCES

*I am uninteresting.* It's a thought I've struggled with at various points throughout my life. I'm sure this thought has a variety of origins, but one contributing experience seems important. I was with a group of people on an overnight trip. We were lying in our sleeping bags, amusing ourselves with a spontaneous game reminiscent of senior accolades. As we lay there, people would shout the name of a person in the group and a "most likely" scenario. Jen is most likely to be president. Tom is mostly likely to win an Oscar. Cindy is most likely to have twelve children. The game went on for some time, and everybody's name was mentioned except for mine. I was not most likely to do anything.

The memory stuck with me for a long time. It led to thoughts that lingered beneath the surface. *Am I that uninteresting? Am I so boring that nobody can imagine me doing anything good or exciting in my future?* At times, thoughts like these lead to feelings of insecurity that impact me when I introduce myself to people. I want to get it over with as soon as possible and say as little as possible about myself, which just reinforces the notion that I actually *am* uninteresting and boring. People sense the anxious energy coming from me and feel uncomfortable in my presence.

One night as I was lying in bed falling asleep, I started to focus on this memory. I pictured the group lying in sleeping bags talking and felt a sense of shame and embarrassment. What happened next must have come through the leading of the Holy Spirit. I asked myself a question. Where was God in that moment? Yes, he is everywhere and was present right next to me, but where did I see him in that mental picture?

I broadened the picture in my mind, almost as if a camera were moving outward to a bird's-eye view of the scene. In this picture, I visualized God as a spotlight in the sky. He was looking down at me, seeing me when everyone else had forgotten me. The potential in my life that no one saw that evening was seen by God. That new mental image is powerful. When I visualize that picture and remember how God sees me, it frees me to see myself clearly and to be my true self. It brings more redemptive thoughts to mind: *I am interesting. I have potential in Christ. I am seen and known by God.*

Changing my thoughts in this way changes my feelings, which changes my actions to be more loving to other people. As I move toward a confidence in the unique ways God has made me, I can start to feel more confident and less anxious when I talk to people.

This helps me to love others better. People sense less anxious energy from me. I come across as less distant or cold, and people can feel more comfortable in my presence. I'm better able to form and build relationships when I am honest about the unique ways that God has made me and feel confident living them out.

Where is God? Where is he when we go through struggle, heartache, crisis, shame, and trauma? He is near and not far off (see Jer. 23:23–24). His glory, goodness, and love fill the earth—and our lives. He is continually present with us as we live out our stories. Our ability to picture this is important. Our awareness of God's presence with us in our past and present experiences influences our thinking about them. We can learn to look at our memories, look at God, and consider what Scripture says about how he was looking at us as we went through various experiences in our lives. This can help us to create more accurate and useful mental images that then influence our current thinking.

## CONNECTING OUR LIVES TO BIBLICAL STORIES

Jihoon was adopted from Korea as a baby and grew up knowing nothing about his birth parents. His whole life, he felt an uncomfortable awareness of how different he was from everyone he knew. As a child, he felt like an outsider in his friend group, and as an adult, he still doesn't know where he fits. He doesn't feel American. He doesn't feel Korean. Each night as he lies in bed recounting his day, his thoughts drift in the same direction. *I don't belong. I don't fit anywhere. I am an outcast.*

His thoughts began to change as he considered the story of Moses. Moses was a Hebrew baby brought into the Egyptian court. Jihoon imagined that Moses must have felt some of the same things and struggled with similar thoughts. Caught between two different cultures, he was never fully accepted as a Hebrew or an Egyptian. It struck Jihoon that God placed Moses in this confusing clash of cultures for a reason. Moses's unique background likely helped him to both negotiate with Pharaoh and convince the Israelites to leave. His unique experience of living between two cultures was used by God as an important part of God's story.

Making these connections did not remove the tension and discomfort Jihoon felt, but it did begin to change his thoughts. Now as he lay in bed at night, his thoughts began to drift in new directions. *What if God has a purpose in this? What if he has placed me here for a reason? I feel like an outcast, but maybe I'm actually called to something more then I realized.* He began imagining different ways God might use his unique gifts and circumstances.

Our ability to move forward into new thoughts can hinge on that moment when we realize where we fit in the story of Scripture. In various counseling sessions, I've seen the story of the prodigal son help people to move from thinking *I am unloved* to *I am wanted.* Stories of David's sin and restoration help people to move from *I am a hopeless case* to *I am forgiven.* Speaking personally, as I've dealt with difficult seasons of chronic illness, the story of the widow's mite has helped me to change my thoughts from *I am a failure* to *God is pleased with the little I have to offer.* Stories from Scripture can replace the faulty or incomplete stories we tell ourselves, helping us to align our thoughts with God's thoughts.

## CHANGING OUR FUTURE STORIES

Addressing our present thoughts by looking at past events can change our future stories. As Jane began to believe that she was worthy, she began to live out of her experience of that worth. She started to see her strengths and realize that her thoughts about not being a good enough parent were false. The more she saw herself as a good parent, the more she began to live out that truth. In my own story, growing in confidence when I encounter social situations can help me to offer people a less anxious presence. As Jihoon explored the story of Moses, his thoughts led him toward ministry within the unique capacity God had given him. Our past experiences are leading us somewhere. They are influencing the nature of our current thoughts and the direction of our future stories.

Romans 12:2 says, "Do not be conformed to this world, but be transformed by the renewal of your mind, that by testing you may discern what is the will of God, what is good and acceptable and perfect." As we explore our stories and transform our thinking, we are moving away from conformation to the world and moving into the will of God. Repairing inaccuracies in our thinking that have been influenced by our past experiences is one way for us to guide our thoughts and stories in the direction God desires them to go.

## A GUIDED JOURNALING PRACTICE
## FOR REPAIRING THOUGHTS

Perhaps you are thinking that this chapter has some nice stories but that this sounds like a complicated process. How would you even begin to make similar changes? Occasionally people make connections between their past stories and present thoughts spontaneously, but more often this happens through purposeful conversation and reflection. Repairing thoughts is a strategy that often requires outside help from someone who can offer a different perspective and ask you questions you may not have considered before. You may consider reaching out to a friend, like Jane did, or scheduling an appointment with a counselor to help you process your story.

If you prefer to reflect on your own, I have created a journaling practice to guide you. It draws on the work of Dan Allender, whose writing has taught me much about engaging the stories of our lives.[2] I have personally benefited from journaling through what Dan Allender calls "memories of influence."[3] These memories of influence include specific times we have experienced hurt and harm and specific times we have experienced encouragement and blessing. By engaging our stories in an honest way, we learn how we have been impacted by both good and bad experiences. This helps us to make more conscious decisions about how we allow our pasts to continue to impact our thought processes today.

Grab something you can journal with. Paper and a pen. Your phone. A computer document. Whatever feels easiest and most natural to help you get out your thoughts. If you prefer not to journal, another option is to take intentional time to reflect on each one of the following questions. Instead of writing down your answer, you can close your eyes and set a timer for two to three minutes and reflect during that time.

Begin your journaling practice by identifying a thought you want to change. What unwanted thought do you want to work on today?

*Pause to journal or reflect*

Hold the thought you have identified in your mind. Where in your past does this thought transport you? Be curious and open to being surprised. Can you remember the first time you had the thought? Who does it remind you of? What past memory or memories may be related to it? Even if you are journaling, close your eyes for a minute to reflect on these questions before you continue writing.

*Pause to journal or reflect*

Pick just one of the memories that came to mind as you considered the origin of your thought. Don't worry about choosing the exact "right" memory. Just go with one of the memories that seems most related. It may even be a memory that seems small or insignificant. That's OK. If it seems related, go with it. You may be surprised how much you were impacted after all. Write about that memory in more detail. What happened? How did you feel? What false messages did you learn from that experience? How do those false messages still impact your thinking patterns?

*Pause to journal or reflect*

As you consider how this memory still impacts your thoughts today, allow your mind to drift to other people and experiences that might help you to move toward truer, more helpful, more appropriate, and more complete thoughts. What people has God sent into your life to contradict the unwanted thoughts you have that are related to this memory? What experiences have you gone through that embody the truth Scripture invites you to believe?

*Pause to journal or reflect*

Go back to the initial memory you identified. Visualize that memory. Describe the mental image in detail. Where would you place God in that mental image? What truths about God's presence and character do you need to hold in mind as you consider this memory?

*Pause to journal or reflect*

One last time, go back to the initial memory you identified. When you think about this event, what biblical story does it remind you of? How might this biblical story help you to consider the memory in a new way?

*Pause to journal or reflect*

Close your time of journaling by considering how changing the thoughts connected to this memory would allow you to better love yourself, others, and God. If you were able to change your thoughts, how would this help you? How would it help you to love others better? How would it increase your ability to live for God in a way that brings him glory?

# Part 3

# SPECIALIZED APPROACHES
## *for Changing Thoughts*

# 9

# SET ASIDE YOUR THOUGHTS

Six months ago, Nadine was robbed at gunpoint. She was walking through a park one night when two masked men jumped out of the bushes and blocked her path. One pointed a gun at her. The other rifled through her purse and pockets. They pulled off her wedding ring, broke her necklace with a painful tug, and disappeared into the dark. The memories did not leave so quickly.

Months later, images of what happened still flash through her mind. Someone yelling. A gun in her face. A hand forcefully searching her coat pocket. Each time she remembers, she feels a rush of fear. Her chest tightens, and she can't take a full breath. She's certain it was her fault. *How could I have been so stupid? I never should have walked through the park at night on my own. I'll never feel safe again. How could God let this happen to me?*

The thoughts and memories consume her. She can't work or sleep. Conversation feels impossible. How can people care so much about the weather and the latest fashion trends when danger lurks around every corner? It's hard for her to focus on things that used to matter. Before that night, she had plans to go back to school. Now, it's all she can do to make it through the day.

Hopelessness. It's the worst part. She walks around wondering if she will feel this way forever. These thoughts are different from anything she has ever experienced. It doesn't feel safe to examine them. She can't pray through them, because she can hardly look at them. The moment she starts to think about what happened, her heart races so fast she has to quickly distract herself to stop the feelings from spiraling out of control.

If you have experienced trauma like Nadine, it's possible that the strategies you have read so far haven't been effective. It's possible that some of them have even made you feel worse. To understand why this can happen, we need to address the basics of how trauma impacts your thoughts. We will then consider how their impact leads trauma survivors to benefit from a slightly different approach. This specialized approach includes strategies to help you temporarily set your thoughts aside instead of immediately trying to deal with them head-on. Setting thoughts aside can help you temporarily reduce the intensity of your thoughts while you gather people and resources around you to help you to deal with them more permanently.

## HOW TRAUMA IMPACTS OUR THOUGHTS

Many of our most persistent unwanted thoughts are connected to past traumas or difficult circumstances that haunt us into the present.

Trauma has been described as an "affliction of the powerless."[1] When Nadine was mugged, she was thrown into a situation of "intense fear, helplessness, loss of control, and threat of annihilation."[2] Traumatic events that might result in a diagnosis of post-traumatic stress disorder involve threat of death or bodily injury to yourself or someone you love. Sometimes referred to as "big-T traumas," these traumatizing events include incidents such as childhood abuse, military combat, sexual assault, mass shootings, natural disasters, and major car accidents.

However, a distressing event doesn't need to threaten death or bodily harm to overwhelm a person's ability to process and cope. Sometimes referred to as "little-t traumas," other traumatizing experiences can include emotional or spiritual abuse, bullying, divorce, legal troubles, financial difficulty, or any significant loss.

A traumatic incident may or may not have a lingering impact depending on how the person who experiences it perceives what happened. The more a person feels out of control and unable to respond during the event, the more likely it is to have a traumatic impact on him or her.[3] After a traumatic incident, some people go on to develop significant post-traumatic symptoms that impact every area of their lives, including their thought processes.

Trauma threatens our core beliefs and "shatters what we believed to be true about our world."[4] A traumatic incident becomes an "overriding" experience, leading to beliefs that "become the basis by which all other information is processed."[5] Before she was mugged, Nadine engaged life with healthy core beliefs. She believed she was safe. She thought she had good judgment. She saw God as a loving protector. Trauma challenged these beliefs and seemed to prove that she was never safe. She began to think she couldn't trust her own decisions. She wondered if God was as loving as she had once thought.

## WHY THOUGHTS CONNECTED TO TRAUMA PERSIST

Thoughts connected to trauma tend to be difficult to change. There are at least five reasons for this: trauma (1) changes the way we store memory, (2) disrupts our speech and language, (3) triggers overwhelming sensations in our bodies, (4) influences how we pay attention, and (5) impairs our ability to make connections.

Memories of trauma are fragmented. While normal autobiographical memory consists of "stories with a beginning, a middle and an end," trauma memories are disorganized.[6] Their details are often forgotten. The timeline of the traumatic incident often feels scrambled. The memories "lack verbal narrative" and instead are "encoded in the form of vivid sensations and images."[7]

Because trauma changes the way memory is encoded, traumatic incidents often feel impossible to articulate. In this way, trauma disrupts speech and language. Some trauma survivors may easily describe *what* happened, but their stories "rarely capture the inner truth of the experience."[8] Words fail to describe the full impact of what happened to them in the past and the extent to which the past continues to infiltrate their experience of the present. Physical changes in the brain explain this disruption. Brain scans of people experiencing flashbacks show that trauma pushes Broca's area, the speech center of the brain, offline. A person with a deactivated Broca's area cannot put "thoughts and feelings into words."[9] It's difficult to change a thought you can't fully articulate.

It's also difficult to change a thought that feels unsafe to look at closely. Trauma triggers overwhelming sensations in the body that persist long after the event is past. Thinking about what happened during the incident or examining thoughts connected with it can bring up overwhelming physical and emotional reminders of the trauma. Intense and sometimes terrifying feelings of guilt, shame, anger, fear, regret, or sadness may surface. Uncomfortable or painful bodily sensations such as a rapid heart rate, adrenaline rush, headache, stomachache, or pressure in the chest may appear. If this is your experience, some of the strategies in this book that ask you to look at your thoughts or pay close attention to your body may feel unhelpful or unsafe.

These overwhelming sensations can influence how a trauma survivor pays attention. Trauma survivors may become hypervigilant, interpreting physical and emotional sensations as signs that they are still in danger long after the incident has passed. Other times, trauma survivors enter a state of detachment that allows them temporary relief from overwhelming thoughts, feelings, and sensations. They may space out or dissociate as the world moves on outside their full conscious awareness. These responses to trauma can make it difficult for trauma survivors to use focusing strategies or to know what they are actually thinking or feeling.

The impact of trauma on memory, attention, emotion, and bodily sensations can impair a person's ability to make connections. Trauma symptoms, which include the thoughts and beliefs connected to a trauma, "have a tendency to become disconnected from their source and to take on a life of their own."[10] A person may be unaware when intense feelings and overwhelming thoughts he or she is experiencing in the present are related to a traumatic incident from weeks, years, or decades ago. It's often more difficult to change thoughts when you don't recognize their origin.

## A DIFFERENT APPROACH
## FOR THOUGHTS CONNECTED TO TRAUMA

The physical impact of trauma does not mean that thoughts connected to a traumatic incident cannot be changed. Trauma survivors, just like everyone else, can work toward thinking true thoughts that are appropriate to their present reality and shaped by their knowledge of God's gracious love for them. However, because of the ways trauma impacts survivors' brains and nervous systems, their approach for accomplishing this goal often needs to be different from other peoples'.

The complex process of healing from trauma goes far beyond the scope of this book. If you believe your unwanted thoughts are connected to trauma, the information in this book won't be adequate for you to face them alone. You need people. Reinforcements. Friends and family members. Trauma-informed counselors. Mentors. Other trauma survivors who understand what you are going through. Gather people around you who understand the impact of trauma and who can help you to heal by using strategies that address the physical, spiritual, mental, and emotional damage caused by what happened to you.

In the meantime, use the previous strategies in this book with caution. If one doesn't work for you, or even seems to make things worse, pass on that strategy for now. Instead, switch your focus to practices that help you to temporarily set your thoughts aside. It's likely you already have practice doing this. Anytime you distract yourself from painful thoughts by watching TV, go on a run to drown out mental noise, or decide not to revisit a painful memory in your mind, you are setting your thoughts aside. One of my goals in this chapter is to help you consider how to do this in a healthy way.

The goal of setting thoughts aside is not to ignore, suppress, or downplay the significance of any unwanted and overwhelming thoughts. One reason you need strategies for setting thoughts aside is because this can help you to ease your way into a sense of safety. The safer and less overwhelmed you feel, the more effectively you will be able to address your thoughts with the people and resources you are gathering around you. Once you begin to feel safer, it's also possible that strategies we have been discussing will start to feel more effective.

The rest of this chapter will offer three practical ways for you to set aside your thoughts.* Don't try to practice all three strategies in real time. Instead, read through them and consider trying one that resonates with you the most.

## STRATEGY №1: GIVE YOUR THOUGHTS TO GOD FOR SAFEKEEPING

God invites us to cast our cares on him, because he cares for us (see 1 Peter 5:7). Many of us would love to take him up on this

---

\* In addition to being helpful for thoughts connected with past trauma, these strategies can also be used for any experiences of intrusive, anxious, or unwanted thoughts that feel too overwhelming or unsafe to face alone.

invitation when unwanted thoughts intrude. We want to take the thoughts and emotions we feel unable to handle, let them go, and give them to God, but we aren't sure how. When this feels difficult for us, sometimes using mental imagery can help.

If you want, you can give this a try now. Settle into a comfortable position and take in a few deep breaths. Then imagine that God has given you a container where you can store all your unwanted thoughts for safekeeping.[11] Visualize in your mind what your container looks like. There should be a way for you to mentally open and close it. It should be big enough to hold all your unwanted thoughts. And it should look inviting. With these guidelines in mind, use your imagination to shape the container. Close your eyes and visualize its shape, size, color, and general appearance.

*Pause to reflect*

Practice using your container by bringing to mind something mildly stressful that happened to you in the past few days. Don't pick anything traumatic. The first time you practice this strategy, make sure to pick something that's just mildly stressful. As you think of the stressful situation, try to remember all the details involved. What happened? What were you thinking? What were you feeling?

*Pause to reflect*

Notice the thoughts, feelings, and sensations that begin to surface. Mildly distressing mental images and mental talk will most likely come to mind. You may notice discomfort in your body or start to feel difficult emotions. As these things appear, visualize yourself opening your container and placing each one inside.

*Pause to reflect*

If you find it difficult to place your thoughts in the container, various mental strategies can help. You can visualize yourself writing your mental talk on a piece of paper and placing the paper in the container. You can shrink down mental images so they fit better. You can reduce the volume of a memory or change the color of an image to make it less upsetting. You can imagine that God is with you to help you when you get stuck. Many people also find it helpful to place emotions, physical sensations, smells, and other experiences inside their containers. Use your imagination to whatever extent you need in order to help you change, control, and contain your thoughts.

*Pause to reflect*

Once you have placed each thought in the container, imagine closing it. Then imagine picking up the container and walking to a place outside your living space where you will leave your thoughts with God. Imagine yourself handing the container over to him. Is there anything you would like to say? Pause to offer a short prayer as you give him your container of thoughts for safekeeping. Ask him to help you to fully leave them with him until you are able to truly address them with the proper support.

*Pause to reflect*

Visualize yourself leaving the container of thoughts with God and walking away. Imagine yourself feeling lighter as you leave your burdens with him. Repeat this exercise of mentally placing your thoughts inside your container any time unwanted thoughts resurface or intrude.

## STRATEGY №2: GROUND YOURSELF
## IN THE TRUTH OF THE PRESENT MOMENT

We have said repeatedly throughout this book that God shows us how to direct our thoughts toward truth (see Phil. 4:8). While our ultimate source of truth is Scripture, we can also remind ourselves of basic truths about our reality by observing our present environment and experience. For example, perhaps there are times when you need to look at your calendar to remember the simple truth that today is today and not the day when your trauma happened. Other times, maybe you need to look around at your furniture to remember the truth that you are in your apartment and not your abuser's bedroom. Or perhaps there are times you need to look at the lock on your door to remember that, at least in this very moment, you are safe.

When past experiences and future uncertainties feel like too much for us to bear, it can be helpful to ground ourselves in the simple truth of our present reality. Reminding ourselves of the reality of our current, right-now circumstances can bring about the sense of safety our bodies and minds need to begin healing from trauma.

If you want to experience how powerful this can be right now, begin by bringing to mind one of your unwanted thoughts. Let yourself sit with that thought for about thirty seconds. Notice how it makes you feel. Notice where you feel it in your body.

*Pause to reflect*

Next, shift your attention away from the thought and ask yourself what is true about your present moment. Begin to answer this question by reminding yourself about a few basic facts of your present reality. What is the date and time? Where are you? What is something in your environment that reminds you that you are safe? What is something in your environment that reminds you that God is with you?

*Pause to reflect and observe*

Next, begin to pay attention to your senses and allow them to tune you in to your environment. What is true about your current surroundings? Look around you and identify five objects that you can see. Any objects at all. The chair across the room, a book sitting on the table, the light switch on the wall, or perhaps a particularly pleasant wall hanging.

*Pause to reflect and observe*

Consider what your body can physically feel and touch. Engage with four things that you can feel. The sweater you are wearing, the feel of the chair you are sitting on, the pages of the book lying next to you, the softness of the carpet on your toes.

*Pause to reflect and observe*

What can you hear? Listen for three different sounds in your environment. Perhaps the air conditioner or heating system is running. Maybe you can hear children laughing outside, some-one typing on a keyboard, or the person sitting across from you breathing gently.

*Pause to reflect and observe*

What can you taste? Engage with two different flavors. Grab a drink of water or a snack and think about the nature of what you are tasting. Brush your teeth, suck on a mint, or eat a piece of chocolate.

*Pause to reflect and observe*

What is one thing you smell in your environment? If needed, go out of your way to find a pleasant scent. The whiff of a sweet-smelling candle, the savory steam of soup bubbling on the stove, a favorite essential oil, or any other number of scents.

*Pause to reflect and observe*

As you finish this exercise, notice how you feel. Do you feel more settled and present? Less inundated by unwanted thoughts? This strategy can be helpful for slowing down your thoughts. It can also help you to become more present if you feel spaced out or detached.

## STRATEGY №3: INTERRUPT YOUR THOUGHTS WITH SELF-SOOTHING ACTIVITIES

When we are in deep pain, we sometimes forget to use the basic tools God has given us to improve our functioning. We forget our basic needs and neglect basic self-care. We are unmotivated to seek out community. We forget simple strategies that help us to rest our minds.

Interrupting your thoughts with self-soothing activities can provide you with much-needed relief while you find people and resources to help you address the root of the problem. If you experience any sort of thought that feels oppressive, unrelenting, or resistant to change, consider making some lists of self-soothing activities that you can use when these thoughts arise.

1. *Write out a list of people and resources that can provide you with support.* What family members, friends, church members, professional helpers, organizations, and hotlines can help you?

2. *Write out a list of places that help you to feel safe, grounded, or at peace.* For example, could you go to a park, coffee shop, friend's place, or specific room or spot in your house?
3. *Write out a list of hobbies and interests that you enjoy.* Do you enjoy gardening, hiking, photography, biking, knitting, cooking, building, or landscaping?
4. *Write out a list of activities that require high levels of concentration or that provide a mental break.* Could you listen to music, exercise, write an article, play video games, watch TV, read a book, do a crossword puzzle, watch a sermon, or listen to Scripture being read aloud?
5. *Write out a list of ways you can improve difficult moments.* If you can't get rid of an unwanted thought, what can you do to make the moment better while it lasts? Does it help you to pray, take a bath, go for a walk, ease your physical discomfort, or visualize the thought drifting away?

Consider hanging these lists somewhere you can easily see them. Let them remind you of basic ways you can care for yourself and simple strategies you can use to tend to your thoughts as you go through each day.

### HOPE AND HEALING
### FOR THOUGHTS CONNECTED TO TRAUMA

If these strategies seem insufficient to help you to change thoughts connected to trauma, you are right. The process of healing doesn't stop here. Your next step is to find a trauma-informed counselor who can help you to address the root of how trauma has shaped your thoughts, overtaken your heart, and injured your body.

After months of worsening symptoms, Nadine sought the care she needed. She walked into her first appointment with a sense of dread. She didn't want to talk about what had happened. And she was surprised when her counselor didn't ask her for details. Instead, her counselor told her that the first step toward healing was for her body, mind, and soul to start feeling safe again.

Nadine took a few months to ease her way into a sense of safety. She learned various strategies for temporarily setting her thoughts aside. She gathered an army of support around her, started taking medication for her anxiety, and began practicing deep-breathing strategies while meditating on the promises of Scripture. During one session she knew she was ready. She finally felt able to talk about what had happened.

Over the next six months, Nadine slowly pieced together the fragments of her story. Her counselor helped her to see connections she never would have been able to make on her own. She saw how her thoughts, emotions, and physical symptoms connected to one another and found their origin in her trauma. She began to verbalize thoughts she hadn't consciously known were there. *I always feel unsafe. I can't trust myself to make good decisions. God didn't protect me. Does he even love me?* Nadine was committed to believing Scripture, but she was left to wonder what God's love actually meant. Would she ever be able to feel the truth of his love again?

It was not a quick or easy process, but as Nadine continued to process her story in a safe place, her thoughts began to change. She began to see how she had blocked out of her mind all the ways God *had* protected her. He had protected her from physical harm and sent a passerby to help her home when she was in a state of shock. She also wrestled hard to understand the mystery of God's unfailing love that endures even when bad things happen. As her body began to feel safer and less activated, she was able to pray again. Her focus improved, and she started to meditate on Scripture. She was able to connect with people again and began to experience God's love through the people around her.

Over a year later, Nadine left her final session, reflecting on all she had been through. *What happened to me was terrible, but just* because it happened in the past doesn't mean it will necessarily happen again. God did protect me, just not the way I wanted. I don't understand why this happened, but I know for sure that God is with me and that he does love me no matter what struggles I face in the future.

# 10

## DISMISS YOUR THOUGHTS

Brian is chopping vegetables when he looks across the room at his toddler playing with blocks. A horrible thought flashes through his mind. He envisions himself walking across the room and stabbing his little girl. He drops the knife. His face flushes red with horror. *Where did that come from? What does it mean? Am I safe to be around the baby?*

Marquis can't be in high places without feeling an urge to throw himself over the edge. He's not suicidal. He doesn't want to die. Still, he can't stop wondering and imagining. *What if I jumped?*

The phrase *I hate God* runs through Jin's mind on repeat. The thought appears out of nowhere, and each time it does, she feels a wave of clammy dread rush through her body. *I don't hate God. I love God. Why do I keep thinking this terrible thought? What if I'm committing the unforgivable sin by not being able to stop?*

Nia has uncontrollable fears about her health. Every symptom seems like a sign she might die. She lies in bed at night wondering, *What if it's cancer? Maybe I have ALS. That rash on my arm can't be nothing.*

Although the content of Brian's, Marquis's, Jin's, and Nia's thoughts is different, their thoughts hold a few things in common. They are intrusive. They are distressing. And they feel impossible to escape.

## WHAT ARE INTRUSIVE THOUGHTS?

Intrusive thoughts are unsettling thoughts that appear out of nowhere. For some people, the content of these thoughts is shocking or surprising. *Did I run over someone with my car last night? What if I hurt my child?* For other people, these thoughts are common fears that become excessive or begin to repeat on overdrive. *Did I turn off the stove? Does this stomach pain mean I have cancer? What if I'm not a Christian?*

Some intrusive thoughts are upsetting simply because of the way they make us feel. *I must straighten those pillows, or I won't feel right.* Other intrusive thoughts are upsetting because they revolve around highly sensitive or morally repugnant themes. *What if I molest my niece?* Intrusive thoughts often feel shameful or shocking to admit. They may involve graphic images of violence or sexuality or revolve around issues of identity such as a fear of being transgender. They may involve fears of doing something inappropriate, such as shouting expletives into a crowd, or committing a criminal act, such as pushing someone in front of a moving train.

I have experienced intrusive thoughts on several occasions. The most notable time was after someone shared with me the details of a trauma they had gone through. After that conversation, intrusive images of a similar trauma happening to me appeared in my mind out of nowhere. It was disturbing and upsetting. The thoughts persisted for several months, slowly decreasing until they finally disappeared.

For Christians, intrusive thoughts can take on a religious tone. People who struggle with this type of intrusive thinking—often called scrupulosity—experience extreme doubts and fears related to their beliefs about God, faith, and the Scriptures. These thoughts might include

- doubts that they are truly saved
- fears regarding specific sins, such as a fear of committing an unpardonable sin or grieving the Holy Spirit, or constant concern over whether certain thoughts or actions are sinful or not
- intrusive thoughts related to blaspheming or angering God
- fears related to specific verses in Scripture that talk about judgment, hell, or other difficult topics

For some people, intrusive thoughts appear only a few times or dissipate after a few months. For others, they turn into highly distressing cycles of thinking that worsen over time and feel impossible to escape. In their most distressing form, these thoughts might receive a diagnosis of obsessive-compulsive disorder (OCD). For those who experience OCD, the persistent intrusive thoughts, called obsessions, are accompanied by behaviors called compulsions that people use to temporarily defuse their anxiety.*

## WHY DO INTRUSIVE THOUGHTS BECOME OBSESSIVE?

Unwanted intrusive thoughts are commonplace. Somewhere between 80 to 94 percent of people experience them.[1] I have

---

* A person is diagnosed with obsessive-compulsive disorder when he or she experiences a constellation of symptoms that include obsessive/intrusive thinking and compulsive actions that are distressing, time-consuming, and beginning to interfere with daily life. Many people experience intrusive thoughts without being diagnosed with OCD. Some people experience minor compulsions without having OCD. OCD is merely a description of a common human experience that is in its most severe form.

experienced them before, and it's likely you have too. So why do intrusive thoughts turn into tormenting and obsessive patterns for some of us and dissipate for others? It has to do with how we *respond* to them. As we consider some of the responses to intrusive thoughts that cause them to persist, see if you can relate. Alternatively, see if these descriptions help you to better understand someone you know.

## Ascribing Important Meaning to Intrusive Thoughts

When Brian had thoughts of stabbing his child, he immediately began to imagine this said something crucial about his faith, his identity, and his ability to safely parent his child. *I am a terrible person. What is wrong with me? I shouldn't be alone with her anymore.* He allowed one passing thought to mean far more than it did. He also feared that merely thinking the thought meant the thought was true and that he was likely to act on it.

Consider another person, Lydia, who had the same thought but responded differently. Lydia imagined herself stabbing her child and immediately dismissed the thought as strange. *Well, that's weird. Obviously I would never do that. I must be watching too much CSI.* She instantly knew the thought did not represent a desire to hurt her child or mean she was an unsafe mother. She knew that thoughts do not equal beliefs, nor do they equal actions or intentions. Thoughts are not always true. She let the thought go and went about her day.

Do you tend to respond to intrusive thoughts like Brian or like Lydia? Attaching important meaning to thoughts is often what makes them "distressing and adhesive."[2] One sign that you might be assigning important meaning to thoughts in unhelpful ways is if some of the thoughts you experience seem to bother you more than they would bother other people. Do you get caught up in thoughts that other people, like Lydia, would easily dismiss?

## Using the Wrong Lens to Evaluate Intrusive Thoughts

The lens we use to evaluate our thoughts plays a huge role in determining whether we will dismiss a thought as insignificant or ascribe important meaning to it. People who fall into patterns of scrupulosity or other forms of intrusive thinking often evaluate their thoughts with "distorted views of God, self, and the Christian life which overly sensitize the conscience and ratchet up the significance of the thought."[3]

These distorted views take on many forms. People who struggle with intrusive thinking often fixate on sin and forget the love and mercy of God. They may feel intolerant of uncertainty or reluctant to live with mystery. They often mistake suffering and weakness for sin and feel weighed down by a need to know with absolute certainty whether a thought is sinful or not. They want to perfectly connect the dots of Scripture so that every detail makes sense. It's common for people with intrusive thoughts to evaluate biblical teachings out of context and outside the framework of the gospel. The perceived threat level of their thoughts grows exponentially as they fear that an unresolved thinking pattern means they are living in unrepentant sin or may go to hell if they can't stop it.

Can you relate? Or are you able to rest in what God has done for you and what Scripture says about you?

## Fighting Back against Intrusive Thoughts

If you *can* relate, and you do evaluate your thoughts with a distorted lens, it's likely your thoughts feel threatening to you. If they feel threatening, it's likely they frighten you. So you fight back, doing everything within your power to push them away and get rid of them.

You may even try to do this using advice I gave earlier in this book. As I discussed sinful thinking, I talked about those times when we need to choose not to go there. Perhaps you have been trying to put this into practice. An intrusive thought enters your mind, and you attempt to mentally walk away. You resist the thought, but maybe you have found that the harder you resist, the stronger the thought becomes and the more often it returns.

Intrusive thoughts are different from other kinds of thoughts that typically respond well to this strategy. But how? What is it about them that prevents this strategy from working? One difference relates to the way intrusive thoughts are wired into the physiology of our brains—an important topic we'll discuss in a moment. Another reason pushing them away doesn't work is because the suppression of thoughts can have a rebound effect. Remember the pink tiger? Push it away, and your mind will eventually be drawn back to it. This effect is compounded when a thought surrounds highly charged material.

## Responding to Intrusive Thoughts with Compulsive Urges

When thoughts become distressing, perhaps due to the responses to them we have discussed so far, many people are then drawn toward behaviors, urges, and repetitive actions that help to defuse their distress. They may avoid people or places that trigger reminders of the unwanted thoughts or fall into patterns of checking to be certain they turned off the stove or didn't run over someone with their car. People may wash their hands to defuse anxiety about germs or compulsively straighten and organize things around them to defuse anxiety when their environment does not feel right. Other times, compulsions take the form of mental acts such as silently saying a word or repeating a prayer in response to each intrusive thought.

In the case of scrupulosity, it's common for people to avoid or fixate on certain passages of Scripture or to repeatedly confess sins. Other times, people may compulsively search for reassurance in Scripture, through prayer, or from other people.

What do you have the urge to do when an intrusive thought appears? What behaviors do you feel drawn toward? What mental

actions do you perform? I encourage you to consider these questions, even if you haven't been diagnosed with OCD. Take a few
minutes to write out a list of any compulsive thoughts and actions
that you have the urge to carry out in response to intrusive thoughts.
Think carefully. Many people experience compulsions—especially
mental compulsions—that they aren't aware of.

Following through on compulsions typically offers a temporary sense of relief. For a moment, the person feels better, because
he has avoided a feared consequence or momentarily neutralized
an irrational fear. However, the more a person yields to the urge
to carry out her compulsions, the more her actions legitimize
the intrusive thought as either threatening or overly important
in her mind. This provides validation that reinforces the intrusive
thinking patterns.

## A DIFFERENT APPROACH FOR INTRUSIVE THOUGHTS

There is one more factor for us to discuss as we seek to understand why intrusive thoughts sometimes turn into obsessive
patterns. Intrusive thoughts are perpetuated by physiological
changes in the brain.

These changes are most apparent in people who experience the
worst forms of intrusive thinking. Brain scans of people with OCD
look different from brain scans of the average person. For example,
the basal ganglia, which "coordinates not only movements, but
also our awareness of our thoughts," lights up abnormally.[4] Areas
of the brain involved in error processing are overly active, while
areas involved in controlling inhibitions and restraining habitual
behavior are underactive.[5]

Do these brain scans represent physical problems that lead
to intrusive thinking? Or does fixating on intrusive thoughts
over time lead to abnormalities in the brain? It's hard to know for
sure, and it's likely some of both. Researchers have theorized that

some people who struggle with intrusive thinking are born with an "inherited vulnerability" to developing these thinking patterns.[6] It's also clear from studies on the neuroplasticity of the human brain that the longer a person fixates on an intrusive thought, the more those intrusive thinking patterns become wired into that person's physiology.[7]

While we may debate what causes intrusive thoughts in the first place, the end result of experiencing intrusive thinking patterns over long periods of time is this: a person's intrusive thinking patterns end up being influenced by disordered and highly ingrained neural networks in his or her brain. While our thoughts do generally reveal our hearts, our physiology plays a key role in forming this category of thought. As Michael Emlet has said, intrusive thoughts "may be more of a spontaneous brain-based phenomenon (as a result of the general brokenness we experience after the fall) rather than a chosen cognition, a true meditation of the heart."[8]

Intrusive thoughts are often signs of physical weakness, not spiritual failing. In making this statement, we need to distinguish between a person's actual intrusive thoughts and the problematic beliefs and distorted viewpoints that *led* to the thoughts. These viewpoints often do represent matters of the heart that should be addressed using many of the other strategies in this book. However, the actual intrusive thoughts themselves are much less important than they feel. Just because you think a thought does not mean you desire it or are likely to act on it. Just because a thought crosses your mind does not mean it is true or that you even believe it. It's just a thought. You can dismiss it as such.

Because of the way intrusive thoughts become wired into a person's brain, trying to take them captive by forcing them away will be a futile endeavor. In fact, it will probably make things worse. Remember, intrusive thoughts are different from other kinds of thoughts and require a whole different approach from the strategies we've explored earlier in this book.

My goal in this book is not to provide you with the comprehensive new approach you will need to address your intrusive thinking. Instead, I want to offer a few initial strategies and ideas to get you headed in the right direction. You can begin the process of finding relief by (1) dismissing your thoughts, (2) resisting your compulsions, (3) resting in God, and (4) seeking further help.

These strategies can be helpful for both mild and severe intrusive thoughts. Using these strategies when intrusive thoughts are mild, or when they first appear, can prevent them from turning into a bigger problem. In mild or early cases, you may find these strategies to be immediately helpful. If your struggle is more severe or long-lasting, it's more likely these strategies will take the edge off your suffering while you start the process of seeking additional help.

## DISMISS YOUR THOUGHTS

I named the chapter after this first strategy because it is the overall mindset I encourage you to cultivate as you move forward. Your goal is to begin dismissing your intrusive thoughts as much less important than you are tempted to believe they are. You aren't fighting a threat. You are dismissing nothing more than a harmless thought.

You can start experimenting with dismissing your thoughts today. Each time an intrusive thought crosses your mind, identify it as such. Say to yourself, *That's an intrusive thought.*[9] After identifying the thought as intrusive, dismiss it by reminding yourself what that means. For example, you might tell yourself one of the following: *It's not as powerful or meaningful as it feels. It's not who I am. It does not define me. It's likely related to physical changes in my brain that I am working to rewire.* Try dismissing your thoughts in this way each time they occur.

Put this strategy into practice over the next few hours or days and notice what happens. It's possible that dismissing your thoughts will immediately reduce your distress. It's also possible that you will find this strategy difficult or inadequate. For example, this strategy may fall short if you struggle to know when a thought is intrusive and when it is not. Some people need the help of a counselor to be able to do this.

## RESIST YOUR COMPULSIONS

Once you dismiss your intrusive thoughts, your goal is to resist any compulsions that accompany them.[10] If you can't resist them, then your goal is to delay carrying them out as long as you can. When you experience intrusive thoughts, instead of responding to them with any of the compulsions you have identified, simply accept that the thoughts are there and then dismiss them as you have just learned. Let me help you practice.

When you are ready, bring one of your intrusive thoughts to mind. Or, if you prefer, you can practice this exercise the next time an intrusive thought appears spontaneously. Take a moment to simply allow the thought to be.

*Pause to notice*

As you sit with the thought, notice the compulsion you are tempted to turn toward. Once you identify the compulsion, resist it. Instead of carrying the compulsion out, look at the thought and accept it. This will be uncomfortable, and that is OK. Sit with the uneasiness and notice how it feels. If you look closely, you will notice discomfort or even painful sensations sitting somewhere in your body. Where do you feel this? What does it feel like? Describe it to yourself as best as you can.

*Pause to sit with the discomfort*

Notice how you are able to handle that discomfort. It may feel painful or distressing, but it's not too much for you. Remind

142

yourself that God is present with you as you face it. Many people find that the urge to carry out a compulsion happens on a bell curve. It intensifies, plateaus, and slowly begins to dissipate. As intense as the urge may feel, remind yourself that the discomfort won't last forever. Sometimes merely accepting a thought and noticing you can handle it is enough to help the uncomfortable urge to start to pass.

*Pause for several minutes and notice what happens to the discomfort*

If the discomfort doesn't dissipate, that's OK as well. See if it helps to take a break from the thought by letting it pass through your mind without grasping at it or pushing it away. You might imagine it floating past like a balloon disappearing into the air or like a leaf floating down a stream. As you watch the thought float by, dismiss it as unimportant and refocus your attention on something else. Keep trying to resist the compulsion, and if you can't resist it, try to delay carrying it out as long as you can. Distracting yourself can help. Find something productive to do. Reengage with people around you. Leave the thoughts and compulsions behind as you get back to your day.

## TURN TO GOD

As you address your thoughts and compulsions directly, I encourage you to also consider how your struggle has impacted your faith. As Christians, we expect to find comfort in Scripture, prayer, and community. This is not always the case for people who experience intrusive thoughts. For you, Scripture may be a source of fear, not comfort. Church may be the place that most often triggers your intrusive thinking. Prayer may have become a repetitive ritual that you use to reduce distress instead of a way to connect with God.

Can you painfully relate? If so, you are not alone, and you are not forgotten. You may feel disconnected from God, but that has not removed you from his mercy.

Take a moment to turn to God right now. Pull away from any repetitive confessions or compulsive prayers you may have fallen into in the past. Instead, tell God about your pain and your sorrow. Tell him how your intrusive thoughts have impacted you. How have you suffered? How has your suffering impacted your relationship with him? Turn to God and ask him for help. Turn to him in faith, putting absolute trust in his love and mercy toward you. You may be helpless to face these thoughts in your own power, but you can turn in confidence to the God who freely gives of his love and mercy to all who ask.

## SEEK FURTHER HELP

If it felt too overwhelming or uncomfortable for you to even try those strategies on your own, this is completely understandable. If that's what happened, here's what I suggest you do instead.

First, I recommend you read widely on this topic.[11] People often feel a great deal of relief once they understand their intrusive thoughts better and realize how common they are.

Second, pay attention to any of your lifestyle choices or any content you are consuming that may be worsening your thoughts. For example, it's common for intrusive thoughts to be triggered or worsened by shows that depict violent or sexualized content. You may find that watching the news worsens your intrusive thinking patterns or that your intrusive thoughts increase during seasons of high stress. Pay attention. Notice patterns. Make changes as needed.

Third, I recommend you consider seeing a counselor. As a general rule, you may want to see a counselor if you (1) experience your intrusive thoughts as highly distressing, (2) spend a great deal of time and energy managing the intrusive thoughts or any accompanying compulsions, or (3) find that the thoughts are having a significant impact on your ability to manage your daily life and responsibilities. If any of these things are true of you, the content of this chapter may get you started toward feeling some relief, but it likely will not be enough to help you to find the extent of healing you could experience with professional help.

If you do seek a counselor, find someone who is professionally trained—and consider looking for someone who specializes in OCD. Even if you do not have this diagnosis, the same principles used to treat OCD also apply to general intrusive thinking patterns. A professionally trained counselor with the right experience can normalize your situation, help you to understand some of the distorted viewpoints that have perpetuated the problem for you personally, and teach you better ways to respond to your intrusive thoughts.

If you are struggling, don't hesitate to reach out. There is no shame in needing help.

# 11

# MEDICATE YOUR THOUGHTS

What story comes to mind when you think of psychiatric medication? Two people immediately come to mind for me: Liam and Ava. Liam had severe depression and was hospitalized after revealing that he had a plan to kill himself. He spent some time in an inpatient facility, where a psychiatrist made several significant changes to his medication. I spoke with him a few days after his hospitalization, and the suicidal thoughts that had plagued him for months had completely disappeared. He looked, talked, thought, and acted like a different person after only a few days on new medication.

Ava, on the other hand, was diagnosed with schizophrenia in her thirties. For over a decade, doctors prescribed her a cocktail of heavy antipsychotics that came with significant side effects. The most noticeable one was a drug-induced movement disorder, which compelled her to rock back and forth in her chair as we conversed.

A skilled psychiatrist became suspicious that Ava had been misdiagnosed. He slowly weaned her off the medications. As the weeks went by, her side effects disappeared, and she showed no signs of psychosis. The psychiatrist determined that she had autism, a condition that shares some of the clinical features of schizophrenia. The antipsychotics were unnecessary, led to significant harm, and prevented her from getting appropriate help. It was incredible to watch Ava's transformation as she discontinued her medications and became herself again.

## THE DANGER OF SINGLE STORIES

I share these stories because my interactions with both Liam and Ava profoundly impacted my opinions on psychiatric medication. Liam is a powerful picture in my mind of how necessary medication is for some people. At times, I am tempted to be overly optimistic about medication when I think of the immense relief it brought him. Then I think of Ava. She represents another powerful picture in my mind—this time of how medication can do harm instead of good. At times, I have feared medication when I have remembered the immense pain and suffering it caused her.

Most people have been impacted by stories about psychiatric medication. Often, our first opinions on this controversial subject are based on real-life experiences that we hear about or live through. What story comes to mind for you? Hold this story in your mind and consider how it has shaped your view.

Many people allow anecdotal evidence to function as the force that most strongly shapes their views on psychiatric medication. Personal stories are powerful. They affect people deeply and can lead them to believe that one person's experience will be everybody's experience. In her well-known TED Talk, novelist Chimamanda Adichie talks about "the danger of a single story."[1] She describes how "impressionable" and "vulnerable" people are in the face of stories. Although Adichie says this in the context of addressing cultural and ethnic complexities, her wisdom is far-reaching.

Many people have formed a single story about psychiatric medication. They have had a significant personal experience with medication that either helped or harmed them. Or they have heard a horror story or a miracle story of someone else's experience. From this single story, they draw general conclusions that often highlight those rare cases when medication brings either momentous healing or immense pain.

## A BALANCED PERSPECTIVE

These conclusions, among other factors, can lead people to develop "extreme tendencies" when they assess the value of medication.[2] People with extreme anti-medication tendencies may be uncomfortable with ever using chemicals to treat emotional and mental struggles. They emphasize the many side effects, risks, and downsides of medication. Or they may claim that medication is unnecessary for Christians, who can find everything they need in their relationship with Christ. They may even consider medication for psychiatric issues to be a sin.

People with extreme pro-medication tendencies push back hard against this mindset. They may downplay real risks that are associated with medication or think that people who have concerns about medication are overreacting. They may overprescribe medication for normal life problems or use it as a quick fix for issues that would be better treated through other means.

In his book *Descriptions and Prescriptions*, Michael Emlet, a medical doctor and counselor, encourages people to move away from extremes and develop a more balanced perspective. Not surprisingly, there is truth on both sides of the debate. Those who are cautious of psychiatric medication have good reason to feel this way. Similarly, those who speak out on the dangers of villainizing psychiatric medication also have a valid point. Medication is not helpful *or* harmful; it has the potential to be either. Or both at the same time.

## SHOULD *YOU* CONSIDER MEDICATION
## FOR YOUR UNWANTED THOUGHTS?

What about your specific situation? Should *you* take psychiatric medication? Would medication help you or harm you?

These are personal questions that should be answered based on an assessment of what seems wise in your specific situation and context. When approached in the right way, taking medication is one biblically faithful option for people who experience unwanted thoughts. Scripture doesn't offer any specific passages that either prohibit or command the use of medication for mental or emotional struggles. Based on this, I agree with Charles Hodges's assessment that taking psychiatric medication is a Christian liberty.[3] If, after careful thought, you want to take medication, you are free to do so.

At the same time, there is disagreement among both Christian and secular practitioners about how effective medication is at alleviating the symptoms of different types of mental and emotional struggles. In short, the statistical effectiveness of medication varies greatly depending on the type of medication being taken, the type of struggle being treated, and the skill of the practitioner with making good prescribing decisions. Taking medication is a risk. It may or may not help. It may or may not cause side effects.

Still, many times it is worth the risk. At times, medication brings immense relief and can contribute to "the nurturing and realigning of the human soul towards God's glory."[4] Medication can cause "biological change that has spiritual significance."[5] As their symptoms improve, people may find enough space to know themselves, connect with their communities, and engage with God. Worship, prayer, meditation, and the ability to glorify God through acts of service often become more accessible when their mental pain eases.

For medication to realign us toward God's glory is a worthy goal and desire. It is a reminder for each of us who face this choice to consider what is driving our decision. If you decided to take medication, what would your motivation be? To accept God's gift of relief? To aid your growth and change? Or would you be looking to numb your pain, avoid your issues, and find the quickest (though not necessarily the most God-honoring) road to relief?

Likewise, if you decided not to take medication, what would your motivation be? To find relief through other, more appropriate means? To address issues that medication might hide? Or would you be looking to avoid stigma, hide your shame, and maintain an idol of self-sufficiency? There are sinful ways *to* take psychiatric medication. There are also sinful ways *not* to take psychiatric medication.

## TWO WAYS TO TAKE MEDICATION

Many people get hung up on whether taking medication is the right decision. However, I believe that *how* you take medication—should you choose to do so—is more important than whether or not you decide to take it in the first place. To explain this concept further, let me introduce you to two people who represent two different ways of approaching psychiatric medicine.

### 1. Masking Symptoms and Ignoring Underlying Issues

Kyle struggled with generalized anxiety and panic attacks that stemmed from a difficult childhood. His parents were addicted to heroin, and as Kyle entered adulthood he maintained a deep resentment toward his mother for neglecting him as a child.

When Kyle entered his thirties, he decided to go to counseling to discuss his concerns. At first, Kyle was highly motivated to talk through his issues. He wanted to discuss how he could improve his family relationships and forgive his mother. He wanted to consider how his past was impacting him in the present and explore his own shortcomings in his relationship with his parents.

A few sessions after he started counseling, Kyle started taking antianxiety medication. Suddenly his approach to counseling changed from motivated to completely uninterested. Why? The medicine had worked! He no longer felt anxious. He felt calm around his mother. This was not because he had worked through the issues between them but because the medicine numbed him to the point of being unaffected when his mother tried to aggravate him or start a fight. Now that he felt better, he had no desire to wade back through the struggles and shortcomings that medicine was enabling him to ignore.

Kyle began cancelling and skipping appointments. As his body developed a tolerance to the prescription, he began taking higher doses of his medication to manage his symptoms. His relationship with his mother worsened. Kyle was eventually discharged from counseling because he had violated the clinic's attendance policy. He left worse off than when he first arrived. Medication had provided him with much needed relief, but in the end, it only impeded his growth.

## 2. Creating a Context for Growth

Compare Kyle's experience to that of Bethany. Bethany experienced panic attacks that would last for days at a time. During her panic attacks, she was unable to sleep, work, or eat. Physical symptoms of anxiety consumed her life.

When Bethany first began counseling, she was unable to focus. She was visibly anxious, fidgeted in her seat, and avoided many topics for fear that they would trigger a panic attack. As much as her counselor wanted to help her, and as much as she wanted help, it was impossible for them to move forward when she couldn't hold a normal conversation.

One day Bethany walked into her counseling session carrying a sense of visible calm. Just like Kyle, she had started taking antianxiety medication, and it was having a powerful effect. Her panic attacks were less frequent and much shorter. Her anxiety throughout the day had calmed. She was sleeping, working, and eating. Sweet relief.

From that session forward, Bethany dove into counseling. She made connections between her traumatic past and current actions. She began taking responsibility for her responses to others, when before she had felt as if anxiety controlled her. Once she had felt physically unable to pray because her anxiety prevented her from concentrating, but now she was actively calling out to God in times of distress.

Before, she never left the house because of her anxiety, but now she was spending her weekends outside—camping, kayaking, and hiking with friends. Spending time in nature was good for her body and her soul, and it further decreased her anxiety. Now that her mind was clearer, she began using coping skills that had been impossible for her to implement before. Deep breathing, exercise, and healthy eating became a regular part of her day.

Each week, Bethany took specific steps forward that would have been impossible for her if medicine had not tempered her pain and created a context for her to grow. Over time, as she took healthy steps and made various changes, she found that she needed less medication to manage her symptoms.

## HOW TO TAKE MEDICATION

Kyle and Bethany illustrate how two people can take medication for the same type of problem, experience the same amount of relief, and end up with two completely different results. In the end, the difference came down to their different approaches. Kyle used medication as a way to avoid his troubled thoughts. Bethany used medication as a launching pad for growth. Together, Bethany and Kyle can teach us about the best ways to take medication.

### Take Medication alongside Counseling

In general, medication should be used in the context of counseling. While there are exceptions, psychiatric medication should mainly be taken by people who are also talking through their unwanted thoughts in a counseling setting. Medication is not a cure. It only covers symptoms. Counseling helps to uncover and address the root issues. Even when unwanted thoughts have a physical cause, there are typically spiritual or relational issues surrounding the thoughts that should be considered. Kyle's choice to disengage from counseling was a major reason he didn't improve.

## Take Medication to Help You to Engage with God

Before medication, Bethany's anxiety impaired her ability to concentrate. So many thoughts were racing through her mind that she felt unable to pray. After medication, she actively talked with God when she was distressed. The same can apply to a person's ability to read and engage Scripture.

## Take Medication to Help You to Connect with People

One of the biggest mistakes Kyle made was to use medication to disengage from his mom. Before medication, Kyle felt forced to engage with his mom because her choices and words bothered him. His uncomfortable thoughts nudged him to act. But when medication numbed his feelings, he didn't care anymore and stopped trying.

In contrast, Bethany found that medication provided space for her to think about her relationships more clearly. Because her emotions were tempered, she could be more objective. She was able to approach broken relationships that had once caused her to panic. She was able to seek restoration where that had once felt impossible.

## Take Medication to Help You to Dive into Deep Issues

In Kyle's mind, his only problem was his anxiety. He felt anxious. Full stop. He wasn't willing to see that his anxiety was only one issue in his life. In addition, he was unaware that while his anxiety was partly caused by physical factors, it was also a symptom of his unhealthy response to current life stressors. One of the reasons he didn't improve was because he was unwilling to address these other issues. Bethany took an opposite approach. Medication helped her talk about things she had never discussed before. She used the relief she experienced to dig into and find solutions to past and present issues in her life that had been worsening her anxiety.

## Take Medication to Help You to Make Practical Lifestyle Changes

Medication can open up a toolbox of coping skills that weren't available to a person before. Activities that once seemed impossible become options when medication provides relief. Lifestyle changes such as exercising, eating healthily, sleeping more, socializing, and being outdoors can all have a positive impact on unwanted thoughts. When Bethany began to do these things, she started to gain some control over her anxiety through natural means. Because of this and the other work she was doing, she was able to decrease her medication over time.

## Take Medication to Create a Sense of Relief and Normalcy

Sometimes medication should be used simply as relief from suffering—sometimes no other reason is needed. At times, people endure severe symptoms for years without a break. When they are finally prescribed the right medication, it works! Their symptoms ease, and their conditions improve. What a reminder that God cares about our suffering and sometimes works through medication to alleviate it. When Jesus saw crowds of sick and disabled people around him, he had compassion on them and relieved their pain (see Matt. 14:14). Jesus cares when his children are hurting. He cares when you are in pain.

## A SHORT QUESTIONNAIRE TO GUIDE
## YOUR MEDICATION DECISIONS

The following questionnaire can help you think through some of the most pertinent factors involved in medication-related decisions.

### Consider the Duration, Constancy, and Intensity of Your Unwanted Thoughts

- For how many weeks, months, or years have you experienced unwanted thoughts?
- How constant are your thoughts throughout the day?
- On a scale of 1 to 10, how much distress do your unwanted thoughts cause you?
- To what extent do your thoughts impact your ability to complete daily tasks?
- To what extent do your thoughts impact your relationships?

The more severe your struggle, the more likely it is that medication could be a good option.

### Consider the Safety of Yourself and Others

- Do you have thoughts of self-harm? And, if so, have you acted on these thoughts?
- Do you have thoughts about suicide? Have you come up with a plan for suicide?
- Are you highly distressed, and do you have a history of suicide attempts?
- Do you have thoughts of violence toward others?
- Do your thoughts make you more prone to causing emotional, spiritual, mental, or physical harm to people around you?

The more your struggle poses a danger to yourself or others, the more likely it is that medication could be a good option.

## Consider How Medication Might Align You toward or away from God's Glory

- If your symptoms were relieved, would this help or hinder your ability to worship God?
- Would this help or hinder your ability to pray, read Scripture, and engage in other spiritual disciplines?
- Would this help or hinder your ability to grow in faith and serve others?

The more relief of your symptoms would help rather than hinder your faith, the more likely it is that medication could be a good option.

## Consider the Potential Physical Causes and Consequences of Your Struggle

- Have you been given a medical diagnosis such as dementia that contributes to your unwanted thoughts?
- Have you been given a clinical mental health diagnosis such as schizophrenia that contributes to your unwanted thoughts?
- Is there a history of other people in your immediate and/ or extended family experiencing similar thoughts, which could suggest a possible genetic component?

The more physical the cause and symptoms of your problem, the more likely it is that medication could be a good option.

## Consider What Other Steps You Would Take beyond Taking Medication

- Do you plan to go to counseling while taking medication?
- Are you committed to reading God's Word, praying, and engaging in other spiritual disciplines?
- Do you intend to work on your relationships?

- Are you dedicated to the process of exploring deeper under-lying issues in your life that may be contributing to your unwanted thoughts?
- Are you open to making other practical lifestyle changes?

The more questions you were honestly able to answer yes to, the more likely it is that medication could be a good option.

## TAKING MEDICATION DOES NOT EQUAL WEAKNESS OR A LACK OF FAITH

Medication may not be the right option for you. It isn't the right option for everyone. It's also possible that medication could be an important piece of the puzzle in your efforts to change your thoughts.

When used wisely, medicine can be a gift from God that allows people to hear him, see him, and respond to him more clearly. Medication can increase our ability to function, which likewise increases our ability to serve, worship, and live a life of active faith. When suffering is lifted, people are more equipped to pray, read Scripture, and receive help from others. They are more able to think logically, trust God when life is uncertain, and process the deeper heart issues that surround and underlie any mental health diagnoses that they might be experiencing.

If you decide to take medicine, move forward boldly. Taking medication does not equal weakness or lack of faith. God can use medication to relieve your symptoms and reorient you toward him. If people have tried to shame you away from medication or con-vince you it is unbiblical, you can put their opinions aside. Receive this good gift. Know that taking medication can be righteous and pleasing to God if you follow after him as you do so.

# 12

# SIT WITH YOUR THOUGHTS

As we near the end of this book, take a moment to reflect. What strategies have you found helpful? Which strategies haven't seemed to work? In what ways have you improved, and in which areas do you still feel stuck?

Perhaps you have found a lot of help in these pages. Or perhaps you have not. It's possible your thoughts feel just as unwanted and just as persistent as when you began, and no amount of effort seems to help.

If change hasn't happened for you, it's understandable if you feel confused, ashamed, and exhausted. It may seem you should be better by now. What are we to make of those times when our unwanted thoughts don't go away?

## SOME UNWANTED THOUGHTS LINGER

There is a common assumption in some Christian circles that unwanted thoughts will always relent if we are faithful enough, try hard enough, and trust God enough. This assumption can seem hopeful and biblical on the surface. We rightly have high expectations for change. We want to hold ourselves accountable to do everything within our power to bring renewal to our minds. We want to emphasize that God is a gracious and powerful healer and to leave room for the miraculous. It is wise and loving for us to have high expectations for relief from our unwanted thoughts. Yet we have to acknowledge and explain those times when relief isn't forthcoming.

When unwanted thoughts linger, people often feel pressure from family members and friends who think they should be better already. At times this external pressure pales in comparison to the pressure people place on themselves. When a struggle to change is long and fruitless, it often leads to hopelessness and shame. Suffering increases exponentially when people start to dislike or blame themselves for not getting better.

If you can relate, listen closely. If your struggle with unwanted thoughts is unrelenting, this does not indicate a lack of faith or trust. It does not mean you are a bad Christian or that you just need to try harder.

Thoughts that seem unresponsive to all your efforts to change them often involve extenuating factors that need to be puzzled out. They are often connected to depression, anxiety, or mood fluctuations. If you saw a physician about these symptoms, they might receive a diagnosis such as panic disorder, major depressive disorder, bipolar disorder, obsessive-compulsive disorder, or schizophrenia. Often there are physical components of these disorders that need to be addressed. Sometimes unrelenting thoughts stem from childhood abuse, persist in the aftermath of a crisis or trauma, or are complicated by physical health conditions. Still other times, lingering unwanted thoughts are appropriate responses to chronically difficult life circumstances or happen in the context of spiritual warfare. If you are in any of these situations, it's likely you will need a counselor's help with the process of changing your thoughts.

God can heal our minds, but he does not always choose to do so. He does not always bring us relief from our thoughts. Some unwanted thoughts linger far longer than it seems they should.

## UNWANTED THOUGHTS ABOUT UNWANTED THOUGHTS

Some unwanted thoughts become an unrelenting thorn in the flesh (see 2 Cor. 12:7–10). We beg God to take them away, but instead he invites us to find strength in our weakness and seek him in our suffering. He invites us to experience his love for us, even as the thoughts remain. Too often, however, we berate ourselves. Instead of resting in the God who is with us and for us, we begin to develop unwanted thoughts about our unwanted thoughts.

Often, these secondary thoughts are identity-focused thoughts. We start to worry about who we are and what our unresolved thoughts mean about us. *Other people handle life so much better. What is wrong with me? Why can't I handle this? I am a failure.*

Other times, our secondary thoughts become God-focused thoughts. We start to question his character and doubt his care for us in our suffering. We are tempted to have "hard thoughts" about God that are ironically more problematic than our original unwanted thinking patterns.[1] In my own struggles over the years, my thoughts have sometimes hardened toward God. I have questioned his love and mercy. I have doubted if he knows what is best for me. *Does God love me? Does he even care? Why does he hate me?*

Sometimes our efforts to change need to shift to these secondary thoughts that consume us. We might not be able to make our depression go away, but we can let God love us through the sadness, numbness, and uncertainty. We might not always be able to stop the panic, but we can believe God is with us even when we are afraid. We might not be able to get completely unstuck from an unwanted thinking pattern, but we can always invite God to sit with us in our pain.

## A GUIDED MEDITATION FOR SITTING
## WITH YOUR THOUGHTS

May I offer a piece of advice for those times when your unwanted thoughts persist and you don't know why? Sit with them. Look at them.* Don't rush to change them. You can't shame yourself into getting better. As you sit with your thoughts, invite God to sit with you. Rest in the God who is with you and for you. He does not condemn you for your struggle or hurry you through your pain.

Settle in for one last guided meditation. Get comfortable. Take in a deep breath. Slowly let it out, feeling your shoulders settle, your face soften, and your body relax. Step outside the train of your thoughts and watch them as an outside onlooker.

Bring to mind those thoughts that just won't relent. They might be about a chronically difficult situation. Or you might not know where they come from. Either way, explore. Let yourself think the thoughts unhindered. Don't try to change them or resist them. Close your eyes and simply notice their presence. You might imagine each one floating past like a cloud passing by or a leaf drifting down a stream.

*Pause to reflect*

As you observe these lingering thoughts, ask yourself how you feel about them. How do you feel about the fact that they have persisted? Get curious. Do you feel anger, disappointment, or shame? Do you feel sadness, grief, or fear? Give each emotion a name. Observe each emotion as it appears without latching on to it or pushing it away.

---

\* This may not be appropriate for thoughts connected to trauma. If that describes your situation, refer to chapter 9 for more appropriate strategies.

*Pause to reflect*

Bring to mind an awareness that God is with you as you watch your thoughts. Invite him to sit next to you. How does it feel to know he is near, watching your thoughts with you?

*Pause to reflect*

Imagine God turning toward you and seeing you in your suffering. Even if you can only manage it for a moment, let yourself see yourself as God sees you. "As the bridegroom rejoices over the bride, so shall your God rejoice over you" (Isa. 62:5). He takes pleasure in you (see Ps. 147:11). He delights in you (see Ps. 149:4 NIV). He quiets you with his love and exults over you with loud singing (see Zeph. 3:17). Rest for a moment and believe this is true.

*Pause to reflect*

Be still and know that he is God. Just rest. Still your body and quiet your mind in the safety of his presence. Breathe in and out slowly. Relax your shoulders. Soften your face. Release your hands. "Where the Spirit of the Lord is, there is freedom" (2 Cor. 3:17). Feel that freedom. Your thoughts do not define you. You are loved by a gracious and holy God.

# Acknowledgments

Over the years, many people have trusted me with their deepest unwanted thoughts. They have offered me their stories and taught me what it looks like for us to courageously work toward resting our minds. Many of the strategies and ideas in this book came together as I sat across from people who allowed me to participate in the process of disentangling their thoughts. To those people, thank you for teaching me about thoughts by inviting me into your stories.

I would never have put these ideas down on paper if it weren't for an invitation from my friend Manda to speak at a women's conference on the topic of taking every thought captive. Manda, I'm grateful for the invitation. Thank you also for being the very first person to offer me feedback on the earliest version of this manuscript.

From beginning to end, this book has come into being because people invited me to explore my ideas further. Dave, thank you for offering me space to talk about this book before it was a fully formed idea and for your guidance in making it a reality. Amanda and Aaron, your feedback and editing brought improvement I never could have achieved on my own.

Many friends were gracious to offer valuable feedback throughout the writing process. Tiana and Bethany, thank you for your input on early chapters in the manuscript. David, thank you for reminding me how important it is to focus on the good in our thoughts and for encouraging me to be vulnerable. Jess, I'm so grateful for your words of encouragement as I wrote and for helping me choose careful wording. Thank you to Minor, Melissa, Carol, and Virginia for practicing the strategies and meditations with me and offering suggestions for improvement.

Many individual chapters were formed and perfected because of people who gave me their expert opinions. Jeff, thank you for offering me your encyclopedic knowledge of resources and for dialoguing with me on what it means to take every thought captive. To my sister, Sarah, thank you for your helpful feedback on thoughts and our bodies. Eliza, thank you for offering your expert review on the chapter on trauma.

Finally, thank you to my husband, Ian, for coming up with the title for this book. I'm grateful for your brainstorming help and constant support!

# Notes

**Introduction: A Loud and Restless Mind**

1. Richard J. Foster, *Celebration of Discipline: The Path to Spiritual Growth*, special anniversary ed. (San Francisco: HarperOne, 2018), chap. 1, Kindle.

**Chapter 1: Know Your Thoughts**

1. J. Alasdair Groves and Winston T. Smith, *Untangling Emotions* (Wheaton, IL: Crossway, 2019), 93.
2. Thank you to my editor Amanda Martin for giving me this illustration.
3. This is a mindfulness strategy developed by Shinzen Young that can be a helpful tool for strengthening your ability to observe your thoughts. It can be found on the *Calm* app, available for Android and iOS (13.0 or later), in the meditation entitled "Untangling Physical Pain."
4. Hannah Anderson, *All That's Good: Recovering the Lost Art of Discernment* (Chicago: Moody, 2018), 30.
5. J. I. Packer, *A Quest for Godliness* (Wheaton, IL: Crossway, 1990), 126, quoted in Dane Ortlund, *Gentle and Lowly: The Heart of Christ for Sinners and Sufferers* (Wheaton, IL: Crossway, 2020), chap. 2, Kindle.
6. See Eliza Huie, "Counseling Conversations | Thoughts," McLean Bible Church, February 17, 2021, video, 3:50, https://mcleanbible .org/tysons/counseling-conversations/.

7. I first practiced this type of journaling after reading Julia Cameron's *The Artist's Way: A Spiritual Path to Higher Creativity*, 25th anniversary ed. (New York: TarcherPerigee, 2016). She calls them "morning pages" and suggests completing them every day, first thing in the morning. Turning this into a regular practice, as she suggests, is an excellent means of becoming more aware of your thought patterns.

## Chapter 2: Pray Your Thoughts

1. David Powlison, foreword to *A Praying Life: Connecting with God in a Distracting World*, by Paul E. Miller (Colorado Springs: NavPress, 2009), 10.

2. Timothy Keller attributes this quotation to Derek Kidner in "Praying Our Tears" (sermon, Redeemer Presbyterian Church, New York, NY, February 27, 2000), available online at https://www.youtube.com/watch?v=DxOWWWVDGD0.

3. See David G. Benner, *The Gift of Being Yourself: The Sacred Call to Self-Discovery*, expanded ed. (Downers Grove, IL: IVP, 2015), 46.

## Chapter 3: Rest Your Thoughts

1. See Sei Yon Sohn et al., "Prevalence of Problematic Smartphone Usage and Associated Mental Health Outcomes amongst Children and Young People: A Systematic Review, Meta-analysis and GRADE of the Evidence," *BMC Psychiatry* 19, no. 356 (November 2019), https://bmcpsychiatry.biomedcentral.com/articles/10.1186/s12888-019-2350-x.

2. See Jean M. Twenge, "Have Smartphones Destroyed a Generation?" *The Atlantic*, September 2017, https://www.theatlantic.com/magazine/archive/2017/09/has-the-smartphone-destroyed-a-generation/534198/.

3. See interview with Tristan Harris in *The Social Dilemma*, directed by Jeff Orlowski (Los Gatos, CA: Netflix, 2020), https://www.netflix.com/title/81254224.

4. Richard J. Foster, *Celebration of Discipline: The Path to Spiritual Growth*, special anniversary ed. (San Francisco: HarperOne, 2018), preface, Kindle (emphasis in original).

5. See Joseph Firth et al., "The 'Online Brain': How the Internet May Be Changing Our Cognition," *World Psychiatry* 18, no. 2 (June 2019): 119–29.

6. Cal Newport, *Digital Minimalism: Choosing a Focused Life in a Noisy World* (New York: Portfolio/Penguin, 2019).

7. See Julia Cameron, *The Artist's Way: A Spiritual Path to Higher Creativity*, 25th anniversary ed. (New York: TarcherPerigee, 2016), chap. 4, Kindle.

8. See Cameron, chap. 4.

9. You can read an overview of the Puritans' approach to meditation in the book *God's Battle Plan for the Mind: The Puritan Practice of Biblical Meditation*, by David W. Saxton (Grand Rapids: Reformation Heritage Books, 2015).

10. See Saxton, 33.

11. See *The Works of George Swinnock, M.A.*, vol. 2, *The Christian Man's Calling, Latter Portion of Part II, and a Portion of Part III* (Edinburgh, 1868), 416, quoted in Saxton, *God's Battle Plan for the Mind*, 38.

12. This meditation comes from Kendall Vanderslice, who writes about the role of food in spiritual formation and offers workshops on incorporating baking with prayer. For more information on how meditation meets the baking of bread, check out her website at https://www.edibletheology.com.

13. See Deb Dana, *The Polyvagal Theory in Therapy: Engaging the Rhythm of Regulation* (New York: W. W. Norton, 2018), 165.

## Chapter 4: Disentangle Your Thoughts

1. This quote is attributed to Dawson Troman.

2. John Murray, "The Nature of Sin," in *Collected Writings of John Murray*, vol. 2, *Select Lectures in Systematic Theology* (repr., Carlisle, PA: Banner of Truth, 2009), 78.

3. Jeremy Pierre, *The Dynamic Heart in Daily Life: Connecting Christ to Human Experience* (Greensboro, NC: New Growth Press, 2016), chap. 1, Kindle.

4. See John Murray, "The Nature of Man," in *Select Lectures in Systematic Theology*, 14.

5. Murray, "Nature of Man," 14.

6. Michael J. Boivin, "Finding God in Prozac or Finding Prozac in God: Preserving a Christian View of the Person amidst a Biopsychological Revolution," *Christian Scholar's Review* 32, no. 2 (January 2002): 170, quoted in John Swinton, *Finding Jesus in the Storm: The Spiritual Lives of Christians with Mental Health Challenges* (Grand Rapids: Eerdmans, 2020), 105–6.

7. Thoughts that originate from the body are still filtered through the heart. In this case it is how the person responds to the thoughts that reveals their hearts.

8. See Murray, "Nature of Man," 14.

9. See Edward T. Welch, *Blame It on the Brain? Distinguishing Chemical Imbalances, Brain Disorders, and Disobedience* (Phillipsburg, NJ: P&R Publishing, 1998), 40, 51.

10. See Killian A. Welch and Alan J. Carson, "When Psychiatric Symptoms Reflect Medical Conditions," *Clinical Medicine* 18, no. 1 (February 2018): 80–87.

11. See Susanne Stübner et al., "Suicidal Ideation and Suicidal Behavior as Rare Adverse Events of Antidepressant Medication: Current Report from the AMSP Multicenter Drug Safety Surveillance Project," *International Journal of Neuropsychopharmacology* 21, no. 9 (September 2018): 814–21, https://academic.oup.com/ijnp/article/21/9/814/5043110.

**Chapter 5: Focus Your Thoughts**

1. See Daniel M. Wegner, David J. Schneider, Samuel R. Carter, and Teri L. White, "Paradoxical Effects of Thought Suppression," *Journal of Personality and Social Psychology* 53, no. 1 (July 1987): 5–13.

2. See David W. Saxton, "Deliberate Meditation," chap. 5 in *God's Battle Plan for the Mind: The Puritan Practice of Biblical Meditation* (Grand Rapids: Reformation Heritage Books, 2015).

## Chapter 6: Capture Your Thoughts

1. See Thayer's Greek Lexicon, s.v. "λογισμός," available online from Blue Letter Bible, accessed February 20, 2021, https://www.blueletterbible.org/lang/lexicon/lexicon.cfm?Strongs=G3053&t=ESV, Strong's number G3053.

2. Thayer's Greek Lexicon, s.v. "νόημα," available online from Blue Letter Bible, accessed February 20, 2021, https://www.blueletterbible.org/lang/lexicon/lexicon.cfm?Strongs=G3540&t=ESV, Strong's number G3540.

3. See Edward T. Welch, *Blame It on the Brain? Distinguishing Chemical Imbalances, Brain Disorders, and Disobedience* (Phillipsburg, NJ: P&R Publishing, 1998), 37.

4. Paul Tripp offers this visual in his video series *Your Walk with God Is a Community Project*, with contributions by David Clyde (Philadelphia: Paul Tripp Ministries, 2006), ten 25-minute sessions on 3 DVDs.

5. See Timothy Keller, *Counterfeit Gods: The Empty Promises of Money, Sex, and Power, and the Only Hope That Matters* (New York: Penguin Books, 2009), introduction, Kindle.

6. My thoughts on this came out of several conversations I had with Jeff McMullen, executive director at Life Counseling Center Ministries.

7. Brother Lawrence, *The Practice of the Presence of God the Best Rule of a Holy Life* (New York: Fleming H. Revell Company, 2013), Conversation 1.

8. J. I. Packer, *Knowing God*, 20th anniversary ed. (Downers Grove, IL: IVP Academic, 1993), chap. 1, Kindle.

## Chapter 7: Calm Your Thoughts

1. See John Murray, "The Nature of Man," in *Collected Writings of John Murray*, vol. 2, *Select Lectures in Systematic Theology* (repr.,

Carlisle, PA: Banner of Truth, 2009), 14; as well as Edward T. Welch, *Blame It on the Brain? Distinguishing Chemical Imbalances, Brain Disorders, and Disobedience* (Phillipsburg, NJ: P&R Publishing), 49.

2. See Deb Dana, *The Polyvagal Theory in Therapy: Engaging the Rhythm of Regulation* (New York: W. W. Norton, 2018), 8–15.

3. See Dana, 50.

4. See Todd Stryd, "'Take a Deep Breath'—How Counseling Ministry Addresses the Body," *Journal of Biblical Counseling* 32, no. 3 (2018): 62–74.

## Chapter 8: Repair Your Thoughts

1. See Amrisha Vaish, Tobias Grossmann, and Amanda Woodward, "Not All Emotions Are Created Equal: The Negativity Bias in Social-Emotional Development," *Psychological Bulletin* 134, no. 3 (May 2008): 383–403.

2. See Dan Allender, "Engaging Your Story," The Allender Center, The Seattle School of Theology & Psychology, accessed May 16, 2021, https://theallendercenter.org/resources/engaging-your-story/.

3. See Allender, "Engaging Your Story."

## Chapter 9: Set Aside Your Thoughts

1. Judith Lewis Herman, *Trauma and Recovery: The Aftermath of Violence—from Domestic Abuse to Political Terror* (New York: Basic Books, 1992), 33.

2. Nancy C. Andreasen, "Posttraumatic Stress Disorder," in *Comprehensive Textbook of Psychiatry/IV*, ed. Harold I. Kaplan and Benjamin J. Sadock, 4th ed. (Baltimore: Williams & Wilkins, 1985), 919, quoted in Herman, *Trauma and Recovery*, 31.

3. See Herman, *Trauma and Recovery*, 34.

4. Diane Mandt Langberg, *On the Threshold of Hope: Opening the Door to Hope and Healing for Survivors of Sexual Abuse* (Carol Stream, IL: Tyndale House Publishers, 1999), chap. 15, Kindle.

5. Langberg, chap. 20.

6. Bessel van der Kolk, *The Body Keeps the Score: Brain, Mind, and Body in the Healing of Trauma* (New York: Penguin Books, 2014), 195.

7. See E. A. Brett and R. Ostroff, "Imagery and Posttraumatic Stress Disorder: An Overview," *American Journal of Psychiatry* 142, no. 4 (April 1985): 417–24, cited in Herman, *Trauma and Recovery*, 38.

8. Van der Kolk, *Body Keeps the Score*, 43.

9. Van der Kolk, 43.

10. Herman, *Trauma and Recovery*, 34.

11. This is based off a common strategy for containing thoughts related to trauma that I first learned about from Jennifer Sweeton, "EMDR: A Rapid, Safe, and Proven Treatment for Trauma through PESI" (workshop, PESI, February 10, 2020).

**Chapter 10: Dismiss Your Thoughts**

1. See Stanley J. Rachman and Padmal de Silva, "Abnormal and Normal Obsessions," *Behaviour Research and Therapy* 16, no. 4 (1978): 233–48; along with Adam S. Radomsky et al., "You Can Run but You Can't Hide: Intrusive Thoughts on Six Continents," abstract, *Journal of Obsessive-Compulsive and Related Disorders* 3, no. 3 (July 2014): 269–79.

2. See S. Rachman, "Obsessions, Responsibility, and Guilt," *Behaviour Research and Therapy* 31, no. 2 (February 1993): 149–54, quoted in Ian Osborn, *Can Christianity Cure Obsessive-Compulsive Disorder? A Psychiatrist Explores the Role of Faith in Treatment* (Grand Rapids: Brazos Press, 2008), 113.

3. Michael R. Emlet, "Scrupulosity: When Doubts Devour," *Journal of Biblical Counseling* 33, no. 3 (2019): 15.

4. Osborn, *Obsessive-Compulsive Disorder*, 122.

5. See Luke J. Norman et al., "Error Processing and Inhibitory Control in Obsessive-Compulsive Disorder: A Meta-analysis Using Statistical Parametric Maps," *Biological Psychiatry* 85, no. 9 (May 2019): 713–25.

6. Osborn, *Obsessive-Compulsive Disorder*, 121.

7. See Norman Doidge, "Redesigning the Brain," chap. 3 in *The Brain That Changes Itself: Stories of Personal Triumph from the Frontiers of Brain Science* (New York: Viking, 2007), for a full discussion.

8. Emlet, "Scrupulosity," 28.

9. This advice about labeling thoughts as intrusive comes from an approach developed by Jeffrey M. Schwartz. You can read more about this approach in the book he wrote with Beverly Beyette, *Brain Lock: Free Yourself from Obsessive-Compulsive Behavior*, 20th anniversary ed. (New York: Harper Perennial, 2016).

10. This strategy is based on one of the most common secular treatments for OCD: as exposure and response prevention therapy. It encourages you to expose yourself to your fears (e.g., people who trigger reminders of your intrusive thoughts, difficult passages of Scripture, and so on) and then respond to them by stopping any compulsions you desire to carry out (e.g., handwashing, repetitive confession, and so on). Research shows this is a highly effective way to begin reducing the intensity of intrusive thoughts. See Dianne M. Hezel and H. Blair Simpson, "Exposure and Response Prevention for Obsessive-Compulsive Disorder: A Review and New Directions," supplement, *Indian Journal of Psychiatry* 61, no. S1 ( January 2019): S85–92.

11. The article "Scrupulosity: When Doubts Devour" by Michael Emlet, cited earlier in this chapter, is the best I have read on the topic. A few other books I recommend include *Brain Lock* by Jeffrey Schwartz and *Can Christianity Cure Obsessive-Compulsive Disorder?* by Ian Osborn, which have also been cited already in this chapter, as well as *Overcoming Unwanted Intrusive Thoughts* by Sally M. Winston and Martin N. Seif (Oakland, CA: New Harbinger Publications, 2017).

### Chapter 11: Medicate Your Thoughts

1. Chimamanda Ngozi Adichie, "The Danger of a Single Story," filmed July 2009 in Oxford, UK, TEDGlobal video, 18:33, https://www.ted .com/talks/chimamanda_adichie_the_danger_of_a_single_story.

2. Michael R. Emlet, *Descriptions and Prescriptions: A Biblical Perspective on Psychiatric Diagnoses and Medications* (Greensboro, NC: New Growth Press, 2017), introduction, Kindle.
3. See Charles Hodges, "Medication: Right or Wrong? Wise or Unwise? Helpful or Not?" Biblical Counseling Coalition, August 24, 2018, https://www.biblicalcounselingcoalition.org /2018/08/24 /medication-right-or-wrong-wise-or-unwise-helpful-or-not/.
4. John Swinton, *Finding Jesus in the Storm: The Spiritual Lives of Christians with Mental Health Challenges* (Grand Rapids: Eerdmans, 2020), 106.
5. Swinton, 107.

**Chapter 12: Sit with Your Thoughts**

1. Kelly M. Kapic, *Embodied Hope: A Theological Meditation on Pain and Suffering* (Downers Grove, IL: IVP Academic, 2017), chap. 1, Kindle.

Did you find this book helpful?
Consider leaving a review online.
The author appreciates your feedback!


Or write to P&R at editorial@prpbooks.com
with your comments. We'd love to hear from you.